Betsy Brittenham is an adventurer, a volunteer and a traveller to over 43 countries. Her passion is helping underprivileged kids learn English to create a path out of poverty. After three decades as an interior designer, renovator and builder, and a decade in fashion, she is dedicating the rest of her life to helping kids in need!

In the sweltering heat of Cambodia, in the crowded, chaotic, dusty streets of Siem Reap, there is an unwritten rule of bicycle travel. To turn left, you simply turn directly into the pandemonium of oncoming traffic, cycle as fast as you can and pray that you don't die! The goal is to cross the oncoming traffic unscathed. The quicker you get over to the correct lane, the quicker your heart rate returns to normal. That is until the next turn. Oh, and look out for the oncoming traffic!

That is what I did with my life. Nothing was going right, so I turned left! One year, four countries, 1200 underprivileged kids…and other crazy travel stories!

To Benjie and Alex, who inspire me daily!

Betsy Brittenham

GOOD LUCK FOR YOU, GOOD DREAMS FOR ME!

One Year, Four Countries, 1,200 Underprivileged Kids and Other Crazy Travel Stories

AUSTIN MACAULEY PUBLISHERS™

LONDON • CAMBRIDGE • NEW YORK • SHARJAH

A CIP catalogue record for this title is available from the British Library.

ISBN 9781528933704 (Paperback)
ISBN 9781528967570 (ePub e-book)

www.austinmacauley.com

First Published (2021)
Austin Macauley Publishers Ltd
25 Canada Square
Canary Wharf
London
E14 5LQ

Thank you to the wonderful kids from all parts of the globe that I have had the privilege of spending time with!

Table of Contents

Intro

I am not a writer by profession. I am an Interior Designer and Home Renovator. Although I love my job, and have renovated over 538 homes, my true passion is helping kids. I have spent extended time every summer for the last 12 years traveling the world and doing various forms of volunteer work in many third world countries. My 22-year-old daughter Alex has volunteered with me for eight years. She has even travelled to countries, independent of me, to volunteer and help kids.

I am writing this collection of stories to inspire readers to "Go, volunteer, make a difference!"

After the breakup of my 17-year relationship, I was determined to move forward in a positive way. Two years prior, I had sent my youngest off to college. I had sold my home, left my best friends of 20 years, closed my Design and Home Renovation business. I had found a great, new home for two husky dogs, and put a lifetime of furnishings in storage. I was determined to make my life and relationship work, in my new location. It didn't work, for many reasons.

At the moment I knew the relationship was irrevocably over, it was only minutes when the thought came to me. Take a year off, *'go volunteer' with kids in need. Learn how to help these kids in the future and be open for all opportunities.* I have not once questioned that decision and have not looked back since that day.

Yes, my friends and family thought I was delusional. My younger sister Molly is a world traveller, volunteer, and a great adventurer. Even Molly said, "You have a lot of Moxy doing this!" I had to look up the word 'Moxy', and quickly determined it was a not the 1970s Canadian Rock band, the Amsterdam artist in residence, or the Norwegian dump truck manufacturer. She was kindly saying I had a lot '*heuvos*' as we say in New Mexico, where we grew up!

As she was driving me to Dulles Airport in Washington DC, headed for Thailand, I said, "What could possibly go wrong?"

Thailand

Chiang Mai, 2017 – The Orphan Kids

On a plane to Chiang Mai, Thailand, with a medium sized, teal blue backpack of simple clothes, a small, red backpack pack filled with electronics, and a stomach full of nerves, I started my year-long adventure. I had just left my two millennial kids, my design business, and everyone I call a friend. I am 58 years old and my biggest fear in life is 'being bored.' Trust me, there is nothing boring about volunteering for a year with underprivileged kids in Thailand, Cambodia, Indonesia, and Nepal!

The Care Corner Orphanage is 14 miles (22km) outside of Chiang Mai, Thailand. My welcoming committee consisted of five young girls and a boy. There were many missing teeth, possibly a complete set between the six kids. Among the mother duck and her troop of ducklings, the meandering chickens, squawking roosters and other strange sounds from unidentified reptiles, I knew I was where I belonged.

The giggly girls and their huge curious eyes wanted to explore every part of this strange, big lady. I remembered two of the girls from my previous volunteer experience here three years prior. When I called them by their names, their excitement grew. My last encounter with them was holding them on my lap encouraging them to eat, and stop 'monkeying around' at meal time!

At that time, I also worked daily and diligently with little Kwang on her command of a few English words. We worked tirelessly on my quest to have her identify parts of her face. Repeatedly, we went over the English words for eyes, mouth, hair, nose, ears and eyebrows. I fancied myself quite the teacher. She was doing great!

On my last day, after a month of volunteering with the orphan kids, it was time to say goodbye to Kwang. She gave me as big of a hug as a three-year-old can give. She had a huge smile on her face. She then proceeded to put her finger on her nose and said, "Mouth!" Six-year-old Kwang still makes me laugh, and she is a joy to her teachers and friends.

My trepidation of how to reintroduce myself to the 37 orphan kids quickly vanished when I grabbed my Bluetooth speaker, and headed to the play area for what we lovingly call 'Dance Party'. The definition of 'Dance Party' being music and more than one person dancing and having fun!

San Patong, 2017 – Watkukham School

Armed with my 'Teaching English as a Foreign Language Certificate' (TEFL), and eleven years of volunteer experience with kids, I enthusiastically started teaching my many English classes each day. I taught about 300 kids from 5-16 years old at Watkukham School, in a small village named San Patong. It is located about 14 miles (22 km) outside the popular Northern Thailand city of Chiang Mai. It is a State School and it is free to the students. The only fees are for uniforms, school supplies and lunch. There are many poor villagers and even the costs of the free school can be a strain on some families.

The school supports the three surrounding villages near San Patong. An inordinate amount of the kids are being raised by grandparents. The sad reality is that many of the kids are not being raised by their parents due to jail, drugs, HIV, prostitution and abandonment. As sad as some of the kids' background stories are, it is a group of energetic, smart, hardworking, talented, happy kids. The 37 orphans from Care Corner attend school at Watkukham, and blend in seamlessly.

There is something completely special and different about each class and each age of the kids. I find each class a challenge and try to find out what they like and what excites them. But like cute puppies, the little ones always capture my heart and make me laugh.

Seven-year-old Pear came running up to me. Pear is her nickname, as most of the kids have massively long, complicated, and to me, unpronounceable formal names. She is a small, wiry, very shy and quiet little girl. She is an orphan and only has memories of the orphanage, since she was there most of her life.

Pear is my buddy and she became more connected to me the day that she was being bullied. She got knocked down, scraped, and was crying in the middle of the playground. I scolded the bully, and held Pear tightly in my lap for what must have been 15 minutes. It felt as if nobody had done this for her for a very long time. Eventually, she re-joined the others and even had a little skip in her step.

I remember the first day I taught her in class, as she was leaving the room, she ran up to me, put her hands on my stomach and said, "Baby!"

I replied, "No, Pear, no baby." All the while thinking...*possibly Chang Beer belly, baby*! After feeling mortified that a seven-year-old thought I was pregnant, I laughingly relayed the story to her teacher.

Teacher Catoon is a petite, smiley, happy, fantastic teacher about my age. She is also about 90 pounds (41kg) and 5' (152cm) tall. She went on to explain that the kids also asked her if she has a baby in her belly. I guess I don't feel so badly now. Even if I lost 50 pounds, I would still be extra big to the kids!

San Patong, 2014 – The English Teacher

I was so thrilled to be the foreign, volunteer English teacher in the local State School, Watkukham, located outside of Chiang Mai. I was paired up with the current, local English teacher, Aay. She was early 30s, nice, pretty, funny and very unsure of her English skills. She was new to teaching, and I learned the newest teachers were handed the task of being the English teachers. I told her I would be happy to give her private English lessons at break times or during lunch.

She happily accepted, as did a few other teachers, anxious to better their English skills. I told Aay that I thought the best use of our time to learn English was to speak conversation English. It was also a great way to get to know the teacher as well as some of the local customs. I started with, "What did you do last weekend?"

She was a bit shy, and started to tell me about cooking, cleaning, eating with her parents. Then she said, "Oh, and I drank lots of beer!" Well, that we had in common! We had lengthy conversations about what kind of beer, how much beer, how often she drank beer. Then the conversation turned to drinking wine.

We were making good progress on conversational English. She talked of how she likes to drink wine sometimes at lunch. Now that's my kind of teacher that needs wine to get through the afternoon! We continued for weeks on our lessons, and she was doing great.

As we became better acquainted, she started to tell me about her boyfriends. "Boyfriend," I said.

"No," she said, "I have two!"

"OK, let's talk about your boyfriends!" We then had many weeks of girlfriend discussions as I listened to her tell about each of the candidates for her affections. I even got to have an opinion. All of this conversation certainly made the English lessons interesting.

When I returned three years later to volunteer at the same school teaching English, we immediately recognised each other and we had a great laugh as I recalled our English lessons of years ago!

Chiang Mai, 2016 – Manny and The Bar

Arizona raised 21-year-old Manny and his school buddy, Trevor, were exploring Northern Thailand and all the craziness and adventures it has to offer. They were on a limited holiday break from College and their jobs in Arizona. Manny had first been introduced to Thailand by his best girl buddy, Alex. They had volunteered the prior Christmas school break working with underprivileged kids in Northern Thailand.

After a hugely successful 'GO Fund ME' campaign, they raised over $8,000 to help many underprivileged kids out, and provide holiday gifts. Manny even dressed up as Santa Claus and handed out gifts. Everybody was thrilled, and Manny was a huge success!

The experience left Manny with a deep love of travel and quest for adventure. So, back in Chiang Mai, Manny and Trevor rented dusty, well-travelled motorbikes and were ready for a day of checking out the surrounding sights. After an adventurous afternoon, they decided it was 'Chang Beer' time, and they were ready for a break.

Up ahead on the left was the perfect looking spot with its neon 'Chang Beer' sign glowing in the dusty window. They had a huge language barrier with the bartender, but still managed to have many laughs with him. After four beers each, and a couple of hours, they were ready to jump back on their motorbikes and head back to their hostel.

While starting to pay for the beer and getting ready to leave, a young woman about 30 years old walked in. She looked extremely puzzled, turned to the boys and said in English, "What are you guys doing in my dad's house?"

The boys were mortified and tried their best to explain that they thought this was a bar! They apologised, put money on the table and sheepishly got up to leave. The daughter said, "Wait a minute." She was listening to her dad, then translated for the boys. "Well, my dad said he had a great time with you guys and wants you to come back tomorrow," she laughingly said.

We should all go on an adventure with Manny!

Chiang Mai, 2017 – Care Corner Orphanage

Care Corner Orphanage is in San Patong, Thailand. It is a small village located 14 miles (22km) outside of Chiang Mai, located in the north east of Thailand. It has been in existence since 1995 and is run by Riky and Le Wa Tan and their Millennial daughter, Jacinth. They have housed up to 85 orphans at a time and currently have over 37. They are the best example, I have ever experienced, of the dedication, love, hardworking, caring and generosity it takes to successfully run an orphanage.

The kids are happy, clean, well-fed, respectful, curious and many other positive qualities of kids on their way to being good, successful adults. Although, there is the usual amount of chaos associated with kids from age 5 to 16. They also employ several older, former orphans to work as staff to help keep things running smoothly.

The Tan family members are devout Christians and raise the kids with a thorough knowledge and practice of Christianity. Church is attended locally on Sundays. Nightly gatherings discuss stories from the Bible, and prayers are said before meal time. They have even formed a Christian rock band amongst themselves, belting out songs both in Thai and in English.

The kids attend a state-run school, Watkukham, located adjacent to the orphanage. The school has about 300 kids in attendance each day from the local three villages in the surrounding area. There is a pre-school for the kids two to four-year olds. Then, a more structured school starts in kindergarten.

The state schools in Thailand educate their kids through the tenth grade, until most kids are 16 years old. It is rare in this school for the kids from this area to further their education with college or trade school.

The local village is not a wealthy area. Many of the stories the teachers have told me about the students, are unfortunate.

Many kids in the local area are being raised by elderly grandparents because the parents of the students are in jail, deceased, working in the sex trade or have abandoned their kids.

Historically, there has been a significant proliferation of HIV and AIDS in Northern Thailand and the area is associated with prostitution and the sex trade. Too many of these kids are the products of such bad circumstance.

The kids show up to school each day as clean and fresh as possible and the day starts with an outside assembly. Buddhist prayers, school announcements and a motivational short talk, from a rotation of teachers, are said each morning. There is a lively marching band of drums, cymbals, flutes and horns. It is quite prestigious to be a band member.

After the announcements and words of wisdom, the kids scatter to their respective classrooms for the day. I was the only volunteer at the school for my several months there. I was challenged with teaching, all 300 kids, English. I loved the craziness of running every hour to a new classroom filled with smiling, happy faces. I was armed with music and several large balls with emoji faces on them and beach balls. My rule was 'nobody is going to fall asleep in my class!' We usually started class with a favourite song on the Bluetooth speaker and a conga line dancing past the other classrooms, down the stairs, around the volleyball court and back to class. Then it was lesson time. I never quite seemed to know where we were in their books, so usually had a front row kid tell me the page number to turn to.

Although I liked each class, I LOVED the first and second graders the most! I call them my jack-o-lanterns, due to their lack of teeth. It was also the shrieks of joy I loved when I walked in the classroom, and the high fives and hugs they all gave me after class. I'm quite certain it's a similar feeling as being a rock star!

Armed with my big red marker, they were delighted with the big star or heart I would draw on their papers as they finished their work. The class time seemed to fly by, as I was off to the next grade, and usually running late.

The sixth graders were my toughest challenge. The sixth-grade class had 26 kids in it. I would say they were 13 of the best-behaved kids in the school, and 13 of the worst behaved kids in the school. I kept trying to figure out why it was such a tough class. I later had an insightful conversation with a traveller acquaintance who was a school teacher.

I asked her what her toughest age to teach was. She quickly said, "The sixth graders!" I felt redeemed. It wasn't just me and my teaching skills. She went on to explain that her experience with 12-year-olds was that they were entering puberty and being sassy and disrespectful was a part of their growing pains. As tough as they were, we still managed to learn some English and played lots of hangman if they were good!

By Friday afternoon, the teachers were weary, and ready for a break. After my last class of little ones, I told the teacher I'd run the class around the play area and get them all tired out. So we spent many Friday afternoons throwing balls, dancing in circles, chasing each other, blowing bubbles and skipping rope.

I also loved the older kids! I helped with after school study and homework time. They would come to their home room class and either do homework, speak conversation English, practice for a singing competition, watch YouTube videos of pop music, or just giggle and braid each other's hair. I didn't care what they did. I was just happy they were interested in coming and just being teenagers! Many had responsibilities at home for cooking, cleaning and childcare upon their return home.

I didn't have much time to lesson plan, but I tried my best to have several options of teaching activities of things they were interested in. There were lots of lists of; my favourite food, activity, sport, animal, music, colour, superhero and more. Many of the kids had access to the school computers and some of the more fortunate ones had a cell-phone. Although, it was fairly rare.

I remember on many occasions, looking out the second-floor open air windows and seeing the beautiful lush, green rice fields. Often there were farmers and water buffalo working in the fields. It was so beautiful, peaceful and serene. It was a far cry from the high school I went to in Albuquerque, New Mexico that purposely did not have windows in it!

San Patong, 2017 – The Night Vegetable Market

One observation that most people don't realise is that the orphan kids do not have a lot of opportunities to go outside the orphanage. For the kids, it is truly a treat to go outside the orphanage for a special meal or activity out. These outings are some of my best memories, as the kids are so excited and thrilled to see the world outside their orphan gates.

The Sunday night vegetable market was one of those fun outings. The kids knew that if they misbehaved, or didn't do their chores or homework, this privilege would be taken away. There was a huge compliance! That was a big enough threat, so there was usually 100% attendance. Watching over 23 kids pile into a covered truck was always a laugh. There were kids on top of kids, with several hanging off the back bumper as they hung on for dear life. I usually had four little ones on my lap.

The best of the night vegetable markets was about 20 minutes from the orphanage. The older kids were in charge picking out, sorting, buying and getting the vegetables to the truck. I could see 26-year-old Jacinth, using the market to teach the kids 'life skills'.

She is an amazing young lady who has grown up with the orphans, and now is successfully running the orphanage as her parents travel to secure donations and funding for the orphanage. The orphanage receives no government funding.

Jacinth makes sure the kids have fun and lets them each choose some food from the dozens of food cart options, as well as a sweet treat. I noticed a particular Grandma taking a special interest in one of the young girls, Pear. She tucked a little package under Pear's arm and put some coins in her hand. I noticed the Grandma looked very similar to Pear. I later was told that Pear's mum had abandoned her to the orphanage, and was from the village where the vegetable market was. Grandma loves Pear, but is unable to care for her. So, seeing Pear on Sunday nights is a treat for them both. For many months, Pear was too sad to go see

Grandma. Apparently, seeing her grandmother reminded her too much of the mum who had abandoned her.

After some time had passed, she seemed to now enjoy going to see Grandma. Even though the kids get back home a bit past their bed time, they are thrilled for the outing. Many of the little ones passed out sleeping on the bags of lettuce and cabbage on the trip home. A big day was had by all!

Mae Toe Village Near the Myanmar Border, 2014 – The Dead Witchdoctor

The true thing about many good travel stories is that, most times, the stories are so crazy and bizarre, you couldn't possibly make them up. I like to say that I'm not creative enough to make these stories up. I have always said, "No good story started with... I checked into my Five Star hotel and ordered a pina colada."

This story starts with, "So, I'm dancing around the dead witchdoctor's coffin in a small mountain village near the Thailand/Myanmar boarder." I had been warned that while lovely 17-year-old volunteers, Alex and Nicole, and I were attending the funeral of the beloved local witchdoctor, there may be some village men who would take the opportunity to court the girls as future brides.

I wasn't sure I was hearing this right, but I was on full alert. As we stepped up to the raised bamboo home for funeral proceedings, I heard the bamboo cracking under our weight. We quickly scattered, as we were twice the size of the villagers, and certainly did not want to damage their home. Not a great first impression, damaging the home!

We respectfully took seats on the floor near the group of other female villagers. We made sure our shoes were off and the soles of our feet were pointing away from the centre coffin, as the Buddhist custom of respect. It was evening and the chanting and drumming started.

In the centre of the medium-sized room, a colourful red, but somewhat small coffin was displayed about four feet above the ground. The top of the coffin had dozens of candles lit and scattered on it. A handful of the deceased witchdoctor's family and friends started to do a counter clockwise dance around the elevated coffin, as well as chanting in their language. It was a sight unlike any we had ever witnessed.

We were told this man was the village's beloved medicine man. He was very old at his death and he was held in the highest esteem from the villagers.

We certainly did not want to make any social blunders or gaffes. Moments later, what appeared to be the 'village drunk', with his four teeth, unkempt appearance and stench of alcohol, was standing in front of Nicole, with his outstretched hand. Good God! What do we do now! Trying really hard not to be rude, Nicole stood up as the drunken Romeo led her to the dancing circle. Alex and I were mortified, and I had to spring into action.

Alex was laughing so hard, and turned to me and said, "Mum, I have to photograph this because nobody will ever believe this shit." She discretely moved off to the side of the room to get her best photos.

I tried to act cool, but wasn't. I followed the mortified Nicole and her suitor around the dead witchdoctor's coffin. I had to chaperone this event!

How was I going to keep this situation from getting any worse than it already was? Fortunately for all of us, Romeo had indulged in one too many rice wine alcohol drinks and ended up stumbling, falling and disappearing from embarrassment! Nicole and I politely rounded the coffin a few more times, then took our places back on the floor!

This was only our first few hours at the village.

Border of Myanmar, 2014 – Make the Rice

Alex, Nicole and I had gone to the 'sister, boarding school' of our orphanage that we were volunteering at, for the weekend. We went to visit the 25 additional kids that went to school in the small mountain village. It was a rough four-hour drive from the orphanage we were volunteering at.

Many of the kids there were not orphans, but lived so far away, that unless they boarded in this village school, they could not attend school. Most did have parents, but because of the difficulty of bad roads, distance, and lack of money, the parents rarely saw the kids. Sometimes they saw their kids twice a year, at school break times.

The kids at the mountain school were really great, smart, respectful, and felt privileged to be at the school. We brought medicine, clothing and supplies from our orphanage and from stores in the bigger town. The kids slept on mattresses on the floor, and they all helped out with chores. This was a very simple but nice school.

We did a home-stay with one of the village families. The family cooked us a special dinner of local fish and rice. The eldest son, Ronla, was an English tour guide in Chiang Mai. He had returned to the village for the witchdoctor's funeral. He was delighted to have us stay at his family home, and the modest fee we paid would be much appreciated by his family.

He pointed to the floor in the corner of a room in his bamboo home, which was on stilts above ground, and said, "You can sleep there. The outhouse is downstairs."

"OK," we said and threw our small backpacks down.

While we ate the dinner his mum had prepared, the balance of the family sat with us and stared at us. Even a young twenty-year-old monk, who had also returned home for the funeral. We smiled and did our best to make conversation.

With the massive communication barrier, I pulled out my phone and proceeded to show photos of our hometown, schools and families. Just then I realised I had been showing the monk photos of the girls in bikinis, and other scantily dressed outfits. Oh!!! I was failing at every level.

When Ronla, the eldest son and tour guide asked if I wanted to 'make the rice' with Granny in the morning, I enthusiastically answered with a 'Yes!'

After a rough, sleepless night on the bamboo floor, using our backpacks as pillows, the wake-up call happened. It was

4:30 am and I had committed to make the rice with Granny! What was I thinking!

After some translating, I was told to get on this ancient wooden contraption that closely resembled an early stair stepping machine. Up, down, up down. A large wooden hammer type thing would drop and pound the rice to help remove the husks. OK, I can do this. I can make the rice. Granny seemed happy that it was me on the wooden contraption, and not her. I'm going to guess she was 'Great Granny', as she looked well into her 80s.

I was getting my rhythm, and for a brief moment felt like I was helping the family out. After 15 minutes, the novelty seemed to be wearing off. Ronla had disappeared so I just kept going. It was now almost an hour I was on this thing. How much rice did this family eat?

I was finally rescued and felt I had done my exercise for the day, although it was only 5:30 in the morning. Then the rice had to be expertly thrown up and down in a basket to remove the husks.

Granny motioned for me to try it. I was better at the stair stepper! The women laughed and apparently, they said, "She no good at this!"

I now have a huge appreciation for rice and will be just fine if I never 'make the rice again!'

Border of Myanmar, 2014 – Harvest the Fields

Hours later, the girls woke up and we ate…rice! Ronla was determined to show us life in the village and I suspected, he had developed a little crush on the girls. He was going to take us out to the fields to harvest fruit and vegetables. He really knows how to show a girl a good time!

As he attached large bamboo baskets to our backs, and we headed up the lush, green, terraced fields to the top of a mountain. We passed a large water buffalo along the way and he explained that he used to tend to the village buffalo and was called 'Buffalo Boy' in his youth. It was raining, but that was no excuse to not harvest the ripe fruits and vegetables.

He showed us the pomegranate trees and we picked them and threw them in our baskets. It was actually kind of fun. We later stopped at a bamboo rest hut and took some time to admire the beautiful scenery. Just as I got up to carefully walk to the lower terrace, I slipped on the mud, and fell four feet into the muddy ditch. I was howling with laughter. This whole day was hilarious!

Ronla was mortified that I may be hurt. But I couldn't stop laughing. With all his 88 pounds (40 kilos) of strength, he was trying to pull me out of the ditch. Meanwhile the girls were laughing so hard and taking photos of the comical scene.

Once I stopped laughing, I explained that I was fine and could get out of the ditch myself. Just another memorable day in the countryside!

If the day wasn't comical enough, we later walked around the small village and half way up a hill to get a view of the valley. We walked toward a working farm and saw some of the workers harvesting bushels of green leafy vegetables, which most likely had no English translation. If they did, the Thai name was usually translated into something like 'springtime healthy delight' or something equally as strange in translation.

We spotted a very young calf tied up to a rope and happily chewing the nearby grass. "Oh, how cute!" Alex and Nicole said as they got closer and closer to the calf.

Nicole started to video as I said, "Be careful, don't get too close and scare him." Fifteen seconds later as Alex tried to hold out grass and feed the calf, he lunged in fright at Alex. She went flying backwards and landed into the muddy grass. The three of us were howling with laughter.

Nicole later downloaded the video on YouTube and hundreds of their friends watched the crazy cow video. It was definitely a humbling adventure for Alex!

Northern Thailand, 2018 – The Beautiful Thai Women

Travellers over the last many decades always had a 'travel legend' believing that the most beautiful women in the world were in Northern Thailand, specifically in Chiang Mai. Travel legend also continues, "Where there are beautiful women, the men will follow." I'm not exactly sure why, but there is an inordinate amount of elderly, out of shape, unattractive, Western looking men in Chiang Mai. Somehow, they got the memo!

The prolific numbers of these older men seem to all have a very young, often beautiful girl on their arms as they proudly parade through the streets. My travel buddies and I were appalled at the sheer numbers of these mismatched beautiful, very young girls, with ugly, unattractive men. We continually passed these unlikely pairs in the aisles of the night markets, shops, massage parlours and restaurants.

I said, "Let's count, in 10 minutes, how many of these mismatched couples we could see." It was 18 couples we counted within the short 10 minutes. Ugh!!! Was the most printable word we could come up with.

It took many more visits to Thailand to further understand the phenomenon. As a predominately Buddhist country, the Thai people are very forgiving and not judgmental people. In the case of prostitutes and ladyboys, it is believed in the religion that this lifestyle is a result of past life experiences. Bad or unfortunate last life experiences would indenture them to a current life, such as a prostitute or a ladyboy. It is not the sins of this life but that of the past, therefore, the people feel that their lifestyle isn't a direct choice.

Another factor, that several local Thai's had talked to me about, is the economic issue of prostitution. A Thai friend explained to me that many parents living in poverty in small villages all over Thailand will hand over their eldest daughter to unscrupulous people, under the guise of sending their eldest daughter to a bigger city, to become a massage therapist.

The intent is that the daughter will send money home to the poor family each month. Usually, the family will be paid an upfront sum of money by the pimp. The younger the daughter, the more money the family will receive.

Many families know that the daughter is not headed for a life as a masseuse. It is a quietly known secret among the parents and relatives, that their daughter is headed for a lifetime of prostitution. If unsure of their future, upon being sold to the unscrupulous person or persons, the girl quickly realises her role in the transaction upon arrival at the usually seedy, hopelessly depressing brothel.

Most of the girls are deeply and fiercely loyal to their families, and as directed by their parents, send monthly money to their families. The girls take pride in knowing that they are money earners and try their best to keep other siblings away from the life the parents have chosen for her.

I still, for many years, remained baffled as to why the young, beautiful girls and ladyboys chose to spend so much time with the unattractive, old Western guys. I am not totally naive. It clearly is a monetary transaction. But a 40-year age difference is unsettling. One local Thai explained to me once that at the parents' instructions, the young girls were encouraged to go 'be the girlfriend for two weeks, and stay in a nice hotel and order room service.' Wow! Mother of the year!

Many young, beautiful Thai women marry older Western men with the hopes of making their lives, and that of their existing children, or unborn children, easier.

With the high levels of poverty in their world, a Western man of 'some income', appears to be a rich man in Thailand.

There is the general consensus among locals, that each Western man is wealthy and wants a Thai woman to marry.

An acquaintance from the USA once told me that her retired policeman brother was living happily in Thailand with his Thai wife, off his police pension from the USA. I have been told that many of the Thai wives appear loving and devoted, but have local Thai boyfriends outside the marriage.

As I spent more time in Chiang Mai, off the tourist route, I noticed more and more Western men with Thai women. The difference is that I was seeing Thai women over 40, with what seemed to be over 70-year-old men. Still the combination was rampant. Not once did I see an elderly Thai man with a younger Western woman.

Months later, on a rooftop sunset bar in Phnom Penn, I was drinking beer with my two new 30-year-old guy friends from Alaska. The guys helped me unlock the mystery that had been plaguing me for years. When I told them, I did not fully understand the Western, unattractive, old man and beautiful, young Thai girl phenomenon, they shared some insight with me. Both guys were very experienced in dating Thai women and were currently single. I knew they had a much deeper understanding than I.

They explained several factors, including the most obvious one, economic security. Many of the young girls are from small villages and from extremely poor families. They have a deep sense of duty to their families and look at this arrangement as a survival technique to help earn money for the family.

Providing money to their families increases their status in the village, as well as the families' social status. The parents believe it proves they raised a smart, good daughter that is capable of income earning. The families usually try to pass off the daughter's earnings as a more legitimate form of employment, rather than sex work. They will often say their daughter is a tourist guide, a hairdresser, masseuse, a restaurant or hotel worker.

Another reason for the age and attractiveness discrepancy is a sense of being admired by Western men, and the possibility of moving to the Western man's country. Many Thai women feel that getting a foreign husband is the ultimate score, and many will go to great lengths to try to make that happen.

A Thai woman getting pregnant and having a foreigner's child is a very common occurrence. There are many mixed-race children in Thailand. These children are called luck khrueng and in previous generations were often discriminated against. In recent generations, they have become accepted and embraced, as their fair skin, hair, coloured eyes and tall physique are deemed attractive and advantageous.

What I was enlightened to from my new friends, was the fact that the young girls believe they will also, be required to have much less sex with the older man, as opposed to someone much younger. I've also been told that many Thai women think the majority of Western men look similar, and they don't differentiate between being physically attractive or not.

Many say they go for the man's kindness and personality. Most of the young girls will play down the age difference, saying they don't mind the vast age difference.

Another observation in the mixed dating and marriage issue is the proliferation of young children of mixed race. Mixed race being, a Thai mum and a Western dad. Having the Western man's child is considered a big score in the Thai culture, in hopes that the Thai woman will have her child and herself financially taken care of in the future.

Google hosts numerous sites of 'Thai' brides seeking foreign husbands. But the divorce rate in Thailand is 39% of marriages ending in divorce. Mixed race marriages and divorces are not tracked separately. In the USA, roughly 51% of marriages end in divorce. The Thai divorce rate is up 12% from a decade ago. Key factors in Thai divorces are work related stresses, financial and social pressures.

There are numerous reports of Thai women killing or hiring people to kill their spouses. In the case of 69-year Ian Beeston, from the UK, and his 21 years younger wife, Mr Beeston thought he had everything a man could ever want. He took his life savings of $530,000 to Pattaya, Thailand, in search of a new bride.

He met a beautiful Thai woman named Wacheerawan and moved to a small town in Thailand to build the house of his dreams. In Thailand, foreigners are not allowed to own land, so he placed everything in his wife's name. After nine years of marriage, she sold off all his property that he had acquired in Thailand, and secretly kept all the money.

Mr Beestoon soon realised what she had done. She also sold off the residence that Mr Beeston was currently living in, which was the former couple's home. Mr Beeston refused to leave the home Wacheerawan had sold. The new owners were anxious to move in. Wacheerawan and her current boyfriend decided to kill Mr Beeston.

He had expressed to his friends in a letter he left to his lawyers, "I am in real fear for my life." The prophecy came true and Wacheerawan's boyfriend stabbed and killed Mr Beeston, and Wacheerawan was in sole possession of all the money.

While a small percent of Thai women come from bars and brothels and are focused on money rather than love, many are not. Many interracial marriages in Thailand do last, and incidences such as scams and violence are unusual. It is best advised for foreigners to take precautions prior to entering a situation where property and finances are involved.

Chiang Mai, 2002 – First Ladyboy Show!

Ask any traveller about their first ladyboy show and you usually get a great story! In the travel world, it is equivalent to initiation into the big league of world experiences. We are not talking about the circus, Cirque du Soleil, Ice Capades, Mardi Gras, Crazyhorse of Paris or even the Macy's Day Parade.

It is a semi-homespun combination of all the above. Most often, the Ladyboy Cabaret, as they like to refer to themselves, is performing at a venue close to a popular spot like a night market. The ladies, as I'll call them, usually walk the aisles of the night markets, pre-show, to drum up excitement and takers for their performances for the evening. These beautiful ladies put 'us born females' to shame! They are extremely beautiful, expertly coiffed and made up. They are beautifully dressed, have perfect posture and big seductive smiles.

They are wearing elaborate showgirl costumes, fishnet hose and very high heels. Each has a unique look or as I call it, a 'theme' to their outfit. Many try desperately to look like a recognisable, current or past pop star. I have seen many attempts at Britney Spears, Christina Aguilera, Jennifer Lopez, Diana Ross, and Cher.

My first ladyboy show was in the night market in Chiang Mai, Thailand. Armed with my 11 travel buddies and lots of Chang beer, we were ready for the Cabaret show. We knew it was a fun, humorous attempt to lip-sync and be the best 'Britney' they could perform in front of an adoring audience. The audience of about 100 travellers was packed, and we all cheered, clapped and laughed at the fun-filled hour and a half show. Oh, and several additional beers.

I had made a new best friend in ladyboy, Sunny, by tipping her/him generously throughout the show, as she delivered my Chang beer to the table. Sunny, was a true relic of an aging ladyboy. Her makeup was extra heavy, with thick, black eyebrows expressively drawn on. She was carrying far more weight in her miniskirt and platform shoes than her younger counterparts. She moved slowly, didn't put up with any of the travellers' nonsense, and seemed for the most part, to enjoy her job.

Nearing the end of the show, Sunny disappeared behind the curtain. Minutes later as the curtain opened, there was Sunny, proudly standing, lip-syncing to an old-fashioned relic of a song. We clapped wildly, as we wondered what her true talent was. She made a valiant effort, as we suffered through her silly song, when at the end of it we noticed her skirt had inched up. Unbeknownst to her, her penis was dangling down from her miniskirt for the entire crowd to see. Oh, how embarrassing for poor Sunny!

The crowd too had seen the same embarrassing thing that we had seen. There was lots of whispering amongst the crowd. I was mortified for Sunny. As she finished her song, someone in the audience was pointing to her penis. She quickly looked down, grabbed her penis and held it high above her head. That was the rubber penis we had all been staring at. That was quite the closing act! Wow! What a talent!

Bangkok and Northern Thailand, 2018 – Ladyboys in a Thai Culture

When most people hear the word 'Thailand', they think of beautiful temples, glittering stupas, bustling crowded market places, an abundance of exotic flowers. They visualise colourful, noisy tuk tuks, hot, steamy bowls of Thai delicacies, push carts serving multitudes of delicious foods and the gentle smiles of the kind Thai people.

Another frequently image that many people conjure up is the beautiful and abundant ladyboys. They are sometimes referred to by others as kathoey. Rarely, do they refer to themselves as kathoey. They preferring the term ladyboy, instead. Ladyboys are referred to in Thailand as the third gender and is defined as a transgender woman or an effeminate gay male.

The term refers to males exhibiting varying degrees of femininity. Many dress as women and are undergoing 'feminising' medical procedures such as female hormones, breast implants, Adam's apple reductions and silicone injections. Others may wear make-up, and dress as women and use the female pronoun.

In the Thai, Buddhist religion, it is believed that homosexuality stems from 'lower-level spirits' that are influenced from one's past life. The Buddhist view is that kathoeys are the marking of an individual who is born with a disability, as a direct result of their past life sins.

Although many ladyboys work in predominantly female occupations like beauty salons, restaurants and dress shops, there are a high percentage working in cabarets and in sex work. There is a high rate of HIV among ladyboys.

Many ladyboys have social and legal impediments. Telling their families of their lifestyle choice and facing rejection is a major issue. They generally have a greater acceptance in Thailand than in other Asian cultures. There is no legal recognition in Thailand for ladyboys. Even if the ladyboy has completed gender reassignment, they are not allowed to change their legal sex. ID cards are required to remain in the male name. A ladyboy, if incarcerated, would be assigned to an all-male jail.

Transgendered individuals were automatically exempt from compulsory military service in Thailand. In 2008, the military added a third category for transsexuals that dismissed them for military service due to 'an illness that cannot be cured inside of 30 days'.

A majority of the western world may refer to the ladyboys as transgendered or LGBT (lesbian, gay, bi-sexual, transgender). The Thai culture has yet to catch up to the modern world of LGBT rights and advocacy, and the majority of the transgendered call themselves ladyboys.

In the film by Vivien Chen, 'The Third Gender: Documentary on Thailand's Transgender community', one mid-twenty aged ladyboy was asked, "Are you a boy or a girl?"

Her response was, "I don't know if I'm a ladyboy, but inside I'm a lady."

Another answered, "My mind is a lady, not a ladyboy." The film describes the difficult or 'bad' social meaning for the families of the ladyboys. Many families shun the ladyboy family member, and reject all family support.

Often, when rejected by their family and village, the ladyboy will seek out the empathy and company of other ladyboys. Many head for the popular tourist towns of Pattaya, Bangkok, Phuket, Chiang Mai and others. When asked, "At what age did you recognise the feelings of wanting to be a woman?" Answers varied, but many said at age five to six years old, they knew they preferred being a woman to being a man. Mostly identifying as female by puberty.

When asked what draws them to the ladyboy lifestyle in the popular locations. The predominant answers were, "A sense of glamour, an acceptability, a chance to make a living, a life away from an unaccepting family and being with like-minded individuals." Most said that the male attention was a great pull, and the feeling of being desired by the male customers. Some found it a great challenge to lure men's gazes away from their female partner in an effort to sexually conquer these men.

When asked if they identify with being a gay male, none of the respondents answered 'Yes'. The ladyboys all confirmed the fact that they were, "Ladies, trapped in a male body."

Many people question, "Why are there so many ladyboys in Thailand as opposed to other cultures?" The answer starts with the Buddhist religion being extremely tolerant of the third sex. Buddhist followers are less judgmental of the ladyboys. In the Thai culture, the ladyboys as well as prostitutes are judged less harshly and are 'felt sorry for'. They believe it is the sins of a past life that created their choices, not from current day choices.

There is also a culture of inexpensive hormone pills, injections and surgeries to enable a transition from male to female. Sex change surgery is relatively cheap in Thailand and due to the great numbers of operations, there are many experienced doctors in the field of sex change.

There are a staggeringly high number of suicides among transgendered people. Forty-one percent of transgendered people commit suicide compared with 16 suicides per 100,000 people in Thailand. It is a bigger killer in Thailand than murder. Some of the reasons for suicide are feeling harassed, rejected by family, victimised and bullied. Exact numbers of ladyboy suicides were not recorded.

The Ladyboy Cabaret is extremely popular and many shows such as 'Tiffany' and 'Calypso' are televised in Asia. There are also many televised beauty contests throughout the year for ladyboys. Several of the ladyboys when asked about their goals in life, talked about the dream of being on the 'Tiffany' televised cabaret show, or winning a beauty contest.

Many first-time viewers of a ladyboy cabaret show are in awe of what they call 'creatures far more graceful than the women they know.' Described as: 'Prowling the streets at night with their swaying hips, perfect pink pouts and come-hither eyes'.

Many a 'new male traveller' to Thailand is lured to the beguiling, beautiful, enchanting specimen of a woman, later to find out she is a man!

Northern Thailand, 2017 –Elephant Feeding and Bathing

In Thailand, years ago, a popular tourist attraction was riding elephants through the jungle. What most of us didn't know at that time was the extent of the elephants' poor treatment in training to perform certain tasks. The elephant's mahout, or lifelong trainer, would jab a sharp object into the elephant to make it follow directions. Unbeknownst to most travellers, most elephants were not treated well, and many were treated extremely poorly.

Fortunately, with internet exposure and education, most travellers now know not to ride elephants, but to spend time in the elephant sanctuaries throughout Thailand. It is a great concept and seems to be mutually beneficial to elephants, tourists and elephant owners. A tourist is picked from their lodging and driven through the beautiful, lush countryside, to one of the many elephant sanctuaries, to spend a half a day with the elephants.

The sanctuaries require that tourists wear one of the companies' colourful ponchos, so it creates a familiarity for the elephants. Apparently, they think we tourists all look similar while wearing the ponchos and it is less stressful for the elephants.

At the sanctuary where my traveller friends and I went, the 10-15 elephants were led out to a covered area, where the tourists were armed with bananas. We were told that bananas are like candy to the elephants! Too many will create stomach problems. The elephants are delighted and eagerly scarf down the bananas.

Often, two big trunks of the elephants are competing for the same banana, and tussle with the person holding it out for them. The baby elephants are just adorable and seem to get a large share of the treats.

After hundreds of bananas are scarfed down, we proceed to feed the elephants, piles and piles of jungle greenery and bamboo stalks.

The elephants can get frisky in their feeding frenzy and wrap their trunks around tourists and squeeze the food from their hands. It always makes for funny photos. After feeding, we tourists get in our bathing gear and traipse through the mud to the local watering hole.

Soon the elephants amble down to the watering hole, and we are encouraged to help them bath in the muddy water. It is a real calamity between the elephants spouting water on themselves as well as on us. We are encouraged to take plastic bins of water and throw it on the elephants to help cool them down in the 90-degree (32 degrees C) weather.

The dozen tourists were shrieking, laughing and throwing water everywhere. Everyone is having a great time! And nobody is missing not riding the elephants. It is certainly a very fun and humane way of spending a half a day in the northern Thailand jungle!

Chiang Mai, 2017 – The Big-C

A trip outside the orphanage was always fun and interesting for the kids. I decided it was time for a treat for the kids and we were all going shopping at the wonderful, large food and department store a few miles away. It's called Big-C and most closely resembles a Wal-Mart in the USA. I have always loved stores like this, as a 'one stop shopping', in abundance. At the Big-C, I am in awe at how inexpensive things are. Jacinth, the head of the orphanage, and I decided that each kid could pick out a pair of new shoes.

We would also get practical supplies the kids needed like toiletries, and school supplies. I also wanted to get some sports balls and equipment, and some snacks for the kids. We all piled into a truck, and were off for an adventure. As a big treat, I bought them lunch at the KFC, as they call it; better known to us as Kentucky Fried Chicken.

I have never seen kids so happy to be out eating at a fast-food restaurant! Their KFC chicken was accompanied by lots of rice and a drink, and the kids were laughing and loving their meal. We took up most all of the seats of the restaurant.

Then, it was upstairs for shopping. We filled the large carts with footballs, badminton rackets, tennis balls, toiletries, beach balls, snacks and some other things the kids managed to slip in. The young girls spotted some Disney princess shoes, complete with sparkly bows and large plastic jewels. The boys were all business picking out their favourite superhero shoes.

We had definitely blown the budget I had suggested, but the kids were having so much fun. As we ambled to the checkout with our treasures, I took a photo of the kids and their faces filled with smiles and grins. Best $300 I've ever spent!

Chiang Mai, 2017 – The Kids' Singing Competition

On my first day of arrival to my school in San Patong, Thailand, I was introduced to the English teacher, Ay. She is a mid-30-year-old, pretty, petite, very smart teacher, with unlimited energy and enthusiasm. I knew we would get along great.

She had an advanced college degree in English, but had no problem asking me for help and the right pronunciation of words and phrases. She taught the bigger kids in the school. Grades 7–10. All the kids seemed to like and respect her. One of my best memories of her is when she was out on the volleyball court in her nicely clean and starched teaching uniform, coaching the volleyball girls. She had no problem jumping, running and serving the ball, just like her volleyball girls.

On day one, she told me I would also be helping two of the kids for the next two weeks, in preparation for a singing competition in English.

"Sure! I'm terrible at singing, but great at English," I said. After school, 14-year-old, pretty, shy, La, showed up for help.

Her friend, and classmate, 14-year-old, Rune, followed. He is a smart, confident, effeminate, mature young man. He could easily pass for a few years older. The two were best friends. Each chose a popular song in English and we practiced pronunciation, clarity and delivery of the songs for days and days. Outside of school, I would find myself doing menial tasks, humming these two songs for the singing competition, and had to shake the ear worms out of my head.

The big competition day arrived. We drove to a nearby school and the kids were ushered into an upstairs room lined with five adult singing judges. I had coached them to do their best, and try to have fun! But they were really nervous.

La stood up, belted out her song with confidence after a slightly wobbly start. She was doing great. Her smile seemed to impress the judges. As she finished, she smiled, bowed and exited the stage.

I hugged her as she said she was happy with her performance. There were eight contestants in each the boys' and girls' division.

Rune, too, started out a bit wobbly. He powered through singing Rihanna's Like a Diamond, like a champ. He too, bowed and came toward us after the song. I hugged him and said, "Good job!" But he didn't look as confident as La.

After the 16 performances of the students, both La and Rune finished fourth in their division. La jumped up and down squealed with excitement and happiness. Whereas Rune was not pleased with his fourth-place performance and looked sad and dejected. "You guys did great!" I said. "Let's go celebrate with an ice cream treat!" It was so interesting to see the difference in attitude of the kids. I looked at Rune and said, "There's always next year!"

San Patong, 2017 – Sports Day

With my middle school and high school kids in San Patong, I was very fortunate to witness sports day! It was a day-long event of football (soccer), volleyball and another local game called takraw. It is a game which uses a medium ball, made from bamboo or plastic that is kicked over a net to the opponent. Both boys and girls play the sport, but usually on separate sex teams. Sports Day was held at a large school about 30 minutes from the kids' own school. The sixth grade and older, had been preparing for a month for the big day.

All the kids participated in a colourful, costumed parade with the other 20 participating schools, to start the day's festivities. The brightly coloured marching bands played their best songs and the athletes carried colourful banners and waved bright flags. Some of the costumes were absolutely beautiful.

Female band leaders were dressed like beautiful Thai princesses in sequin and satin costumes. My favourite was the school that created six dresses for the girls out of bright-blue milk cartons. That won my creative award! There was also the group of kids dressed in 'No Smoking' hats and cigarette costumes.

Other kids surrounded the chosen 10 kids from my school, who were dressed in traditional Thai costumes. These kids were carrying a platform containing a large, reverent photo of the Thai king. In Thailand, the school and religion are mixed in celebrations.

The soccer games started and each school cheered their teammates on with great school pride. It was a carnival like atmosphere with lots of sweet treats, snacks, drinks and trinkets to buy. It was my first introduction to takraw, and the girls as well as boys got to participate.

The teams did great! As the day ended, I could see it was a great success by all the happy smiles, giggling and songs from the kids in the tuk tuk trucks on the way back home!

There are many instances where schoolkids' activities are universal!

Northern Thailand, 2000 – The Raft

On a first trip to Thailand, I was excited to experience all that Thailand and the jungles of northern Thailand had to offer. I had heard legendary stories from my sister, Molly, the great world traveller, of all the exoticism and cool day trips to take.

At that time, riding elephants was not politically incorrect, and we were unaware that some elephants were treated with extremely cruelty. After a fun morning riding elephants in the jungle with my two new, early 20s, German travel buddies, we were then ready for our next adventure. A bamboo rafting trip down the Mae Ping River.

As we arrived at the narrow, winding, muddy looking Mae Ping River, a young, very slight Thai man approached us. He pointed and motioned us to go down the river bank and he would be there soon. The three of us did as we were told and waited patiently by the muddy river bank. We saw on the river bank, what we presumed to be our bamboo raft that would carry us for the next two hours, down the slow-moving muddy river.

It was all of ours first ride on such a crude, simplistic boat. And calling it a boat is definitely a stretch. I'd call it more of 20' (six metres) of bamboo length by about 3' (one metre) wide, periodically held together with some kind of jungle plant string. It was definitely not a seaworthy looking vessel!

So our small, slightly built, young Thai, rafting pilot asked where we were from. After the Germans answered, I said, "I'm from the USA."

"OOOOH!!!" he laughed, "John Wayne!!!" He cocked his fists in a gun pose and started shooting the sky.

"Well, I'm not John Wayne, but that's what I'm going to call you," I said.

We all smiled at each other and slid onto the raft for our ride. John Wayne was absorbed in his thoughts of shooting the bad guys.

The river was moving swiftly, and John Wayne seemed to be proficient at getting us down the river with his long bamboo pole navigating the floor of the river.

To say that we had a rudder to help would have been wishful thinking. All seemed to go well for about 30 minutes. What could possibly go wrong?

That was until our trusty raft started sinking. "Oh, oh, oh, oh," said John Wayne. "We no good!" He continued shaking his head as he frantically tried to manoeuvre us somewhat close to the shore.

"No shit, we're sinking," the three of us said! In a scuffle of a few minutes, we managed to keep our cameras and backpacks above water, as we were shoulder deep in the water, trying to hold onto part of our un-seaworthy bamboo raft.

"I be back!" was all John Wayne had to say upon our landing on the shore, and he was gone. My German friends and I had high hopes we would see John Wayne soon.

Fortunately, their English was far better than my non-existent German and we started to ask each other questions and get to know each other. They also mentioned how they were so glad that they were taking their malaria pills due to all the mosquitoes and crazy bugs and critters in the jungle. Oh, I knew I forgot something! Somehow the malaria pills slipped my mind while packing.

An hour went by in the 94-degree (34 degrees C) jungle with at least that much humidity. Then another hour went by. At this time, I had offered up, "Is this where they kill the tourists?" We were all thinking it, but somehow, I felt the urge to say it. There was a high likelihood it may be a while before someone could find us. I could see the worry on the German's faces. And they could feel my nervousness too.

"Wait! Up-river. Do you guys see what I see?" I said. I was never happier to see John Wayne than at that moment! He was commandeering a slightly bigger, but seaworthy, bamboo raft. He approached us, smiled and said, "Solly, let's go!" Oh yeah! We were not going to die! And I'd just have to wait and see if I have malaria!

San Patong, 2014–2017 – The Health Issues

Six years ago, while first volunteering at Care Corner Orphanage, there were about eight kids who were HIV positive. HIV was first reported in Thailand in 1984, and over 1.2 million cases have been reported. Over half of those people have died from the disease, or complications from HIV.

After sub-Saharan Africa, Thailand is the region with the largest numbers of AIDS-related illnesses. Thailand is the first country to effectively eliminate mother to child transmission of AIDS, at least down to a 2% transmission rate.

Thailand has 9% of the HIV cases in Asia Pacific and hopes to eradicate AIDS by 2030. In 2016, 450,000 Thai people were living with HIV. 16,000 of those people died that year. The Thai government has a 69% rate of medical treatment for people living with HIV. 92% of Thailand's efforts to help HIV infected people are government funded.

Although 50% of HIV is traced to male-on-male sexual contact, 22% is transmitted through sex workers and IV drug usage. The Chiang Mai region, in the north of Thailand is notorious for sex workers and IV drug use.

The HIV infected kids I spent time with in 2012, were products of their mothers carrying the disease, and passing it onto their child. Although, some of the kids lived a relatively normal existence, there were bouts of hospitalisations, constant medication, exhaustion, weak immune system and overall poor health.

The HIV positive kids tried their best to attend school, play some games and sports, and try to lead a normal life. The best experience was watching how loving and caring the other kids were to the sickly kids. It was not unusual to have one or two of the kids in the hospital at the same time for illnesses due to their HIV. It was not uncommon to get the Care Corner Orphanage's monthly newsletter, acknowledging the death of one of the kids from their illness.

The hospitals in Thailand are unlike my experiences with Western hospitals. In the local Thai hospital, near San Patong, there were about 20 ill patients in a room in their hospital beds. No curtains separated the people, and almost each ill person had a family member sitting with them, part or most of the day.

There is no food provided by the hospital for the patient. Any medicine required for the ill person, the family member must go and purchase. Hospital fees must also be paid upon the patient release.

This is very different from most Western cultures, and the hospitalisation fees are a far less money than in Western cultures.

Returning to the orphanage six years later, the few HIV kids there seemed very healthy, vibrant and were indistinguishable from the other kids. I was told that the HIV kids took several pills a day and led mostly normal lives. One of the girls I knew from my first visit who is HIV positive, is now 23 years old, has a husband and an infant daughter who is HIV free. She is a wonderful staff member and a joy to be around!

San Patong, 2014 – The Banners

The very nice thing about volunteering is that 99% of the time everyone is extremely happy to see you every day! There is a high likelihood that the enthusiasm comes from the fact that we bring balls, games, sparkly stuff, bubbles, silly string and an assortment of other cool stuff on a daily basis.

I generally use the cool stuff as bribes, and just as in my many years of parenting, it has a high rate of effectiveness. Most of the places we volunteer at have few school supplies, so the idea of getting a new pencil, notebook, eraser, workbook or cool art supplies is quite exciting.

To the teachers and 300 students, at Watkukham school, we were like rock stars! They don't get many volunteer teachers, and they felt we had a much better command of the English language than they did.

Watkukham is a good example of a state-run school. Uniforms are a requirement. Each morning there is a band procession, prayers, announcements and a moral or ethical discussion for the students, from a rotation of teachers. The school has a nursery and has students up through 10th grade, which is the end of a Thai child's free education.

As 17-year-old Alex and Nicole and I started our first day, they placed the girls with the first and second graders. This was Nicole's first volunteer teaching experience, and she jumped right in and team taught with Alex. I told Nicole it would get easier each day and she would actually be sad to leave at the end of our volunteer month.

The school principle seemed to be happy to have us, and there was even someone taking photos that first day. We felt special. We were dressed modestly in our ankle length sarongs and covered shoulders. But I did notice that Alex had her 'WU-TANG' T-shirt on and Nicole's T-shirt had a large photo of 'Biggie Smalls' with his name labelled proudly under his face.

The next day after the morning meeting, as we were rushing to class, we spotted a large display in front of the principal's office. How nice that they had a display, featuring our photos as the volunteers for the month. We felt really appreciated.

After class as we would walk around the small village, we would get lots of smiles, waves and hellos from the families of the kids we were teaching. The families of the kids were happy that we were teaching their children English. About a week later, we were in a car coming back from a weekend of exploring nearby Chiang Mai, we saw from a distance a large, and I mean 12' long, 4' high (3.8 x 1.3 metres) banner of US!!! WU-TANG and BIGGIE SMALLS shirts and all!

We had to stop the car! If it's possible to be embarrassed, shocked, mortified, horrified, surprised and laughing at the same time, we were! This means everyone who went down this busy road saw this banner.

Oh! This was not the only banner in the town. There were two more attached to the front and back of the school, just to make sure everybody knew who we were. We felt like Celine Dion in her Las Vegas residency!

We eventually got over the shock and carried on with the teaching at hand. At the end of the month, Alex and I begged the principle to let us take one of the posters back to the USA. Alex and I had a devious plan.

A month after our return to the USA, we were visiting Nicole in her beautiful new apartment at the University of Arizona, in Tucson. She had two nice roommates who agreed to let us in a few minutes early before we were to meet Nicole.

Armed with duct tape and the 12' (3.8 metre) Thailand banner, we proudly hung it in the living room above the girls' new sofa. It took a few minutes for the roommates to realise this was a joke. The look on Nicole's face when she walked in, was a re-enactment of the shock, horror, embarrassment and laughter she felt in Thailand.

I'm not sure how long the famous WU-TANG and BIGGIE SMALLS banner of us lasted on the wall in the college apartment, but we certainly did get a lot of laughs out of it!

Cambodia

Siem Reap, 2018 – Orphans and Underprivileged Kids

The kids I've volunteered with are bright, happy, sweet, gregarious, mischievous, loving and sometimes misbehaving. In that sense, they are like other kids in the world that I have ever experienced. My observations of the, over 1,200 kids I had the privilege of knowing this year, is that these underprivileged kids do not seem to have big hopes and dreams for the future. This is unlike the many privileged kids I have known in the USA.

There is a sense of just 'getting through the day', with little to no talk about the future. The majority of these kids will finish their education at about the eighth to the tenth-grade level and will be considered a working adult at about age 16. There is almost no talk of college or further technical training. Many of these kids have already far surpassed their parent's education level.

If the kids are lucky enough to have parents, they will help the parents out with their trade, mini shop, farming or childcare of siblings. There is a deep cultural sense of duty, tradition and loyalty to the family. Many of the orphans after school age, get paying jobs as staff at the orphanage. Others work in a trade that, often, the orphanage has helped to organise.

I remember innocently asking the six-year-olds in class in my best 'toddler level' Khmer, the Cambodian Language, "What did you do over the weekend?"

Little Rattana answered, "I helped my mum do housework and watched my little brother and sister." Rattana is number eight of ten kids in her family. They are extremely poor. She and her siblings are regulars at the free lunch program at school. Rattana's story is not unusual.

I remember taking an exercise walk through the outlying village one day. There I saw two of my six and eight-year-old students at the community water well, doing the family laundry. We waved and smiled at each other. I tried to not show my look of horror on my face. None of this is out of the ordinary in these families. There is a deep sense of family loyalty and sharing responsibilities for the household.

I would laugh and smile at the kids eating the school supplied 'free lunch' and started to call them the 'Lunch Bunch'. They all thought that sounded funny and giggled and laughed every day when I asked how my 'Lunch Bunch' buddies were doing.

Little Rattana was a very shy, smart, quiet, helpful, small six-year-old, who would usually stand by the side of the class before school. She loved to listen to the music we played each morning and she would watch the other kids kicking, hitting and throwing the balls. She never participated in the fun that was going on. She was just too shy and timid.

One day, I enticed her over to me to learn how to throw a ball. Tentatively, she gave it a few tries. A bit rough at first, then day three she showed up a bit earlier, grabbed a ball and joined in all the before school fun. It was so great to see her have some fun. No six-year-old should have to act like a grown up. It robs them of their childhood. But that is the reality of a poor child. It breaks my heart to see some of the very young kids and orphans doing their own laundry.

The best we adults can do is to provide them a safe, loving place to be a kid, and hope they do not have grown up responsibilities as a child at home.

Siem Reap, 2018 – The Kids of Grace House

In Siem Reap, Cambodia, around 300 kids a day are privileged to attend the morning or afternoon English school of Grace House Community Centre. It is, in my opinion, the best run and most effective NGO organisation I have ever witnessed. They help not only underprivileged kids, but their families also. It is a privilege for each kid to spend half their day there, as the state school is only a half a day program for the Cambodian kids.

For a family to be able to have their kid or kids attend, the parents agree to rules including: no begging or solicitation of any kind to foreigners in the nearby Siem Reap, regular attendance, participation and good behaviour in class.

The kids understand these rules and as a result, I find the kids, ranging in age four up to 17, exemplary in behaviour. They have a deep sense of appreciation. I have only heard of a few disruptive kids being asked to leave the program. Most of the students are from homes in the three nearby villages. Many do not have running water or toilet facilities in the home. The toilets are often a small outbuilding. Usually, their electricity is not much more than a light bulb and there are no luxuries like a TV, in the household.

These are kids that walk to school every day, or are maybe lucky enough to ride on the back of a sibling's rusty bicycle. No uniforms are required for Grace House School, unlike the state school, so kids come to school in comfortable play clothes. That made my job of learning the kids' names easier when some kids would wear the same clothes for days at a time. Bopha, 'Oh yeah' red T-shirt with angry birds on it. Dara, yellow soccer jersey. Kolab, pink ragged Barbie shirt.

My other trick in learning the kids' names is to have them sign their classwork and artwork. I put it up in the room close by their chair to help me remember. Once, three of the boys had attended a family funeral, and adhering to local tradition, the parents shaved the young boys' heads. They looked so different bald! I mixed those boys names up for two weeks until their hair started to grow back.

I am so impressed with the kids' ability to pick up English so quickly and rarely had trouble communicating with them. The kids in my classes were so full of life, energy, curiosity and adventure. It also was not unusual throughout the day to chase chickens, roosters and the occasional dog or cat out of the classroom.

Artwork day was always fun. I learned to start with a basic concept and let it rip from there. I made sure I brought lots of supplies from a local book store, to expose the kids to material that they don't usually encounter. I would try to get imaginative and find creative ways to explain and teach subjects.

For teeth brushing, I had them blow up balloons which we called 'balloon buddies'. They drew faces, and connected balloon hands and feet with ribbon. They had to name their balloon buddy, then teach their buddy how to correctly brush their teeth. It was hilarious watching them instruct their new friends.

Another day, I brought a large pad of paper and the kids did life-size drawings of themselves. The detail was so good, and the kids happily paraded their work around the play area. 'Bug artwork day' was great as the kids created their favourite ladybugs, bees, dragonflies and wasps.

It quickly turned hilarious as I cut out a black moustache and taped it to one of the girl's upper lip. Then, another wanted a moustache. Soon, I had a classroom full of eight-year-old kids who looked like Borat, if not their grandfathers!

The success of the school is evident in its wonderful, young, energetic, smart and caring teachers. There were six bright young teachers that had been my students six years prior, on my last volunteer time spent at the school. It is the best example of a program that works seamlessly.

The school helps the students that have graduated, with money and support for a college education. The young graduates then come back to the school as teachers. They are very familiar with the program and I think in some way feel indebted to the school for their education. The young teachers are quickly employed and get teaching experience. The kids respect and are familiar with the teachers, as they are mostly from the surrounding three villages. It gives the young kids a sense of comfort. I have the utmost respect for Grace House Community Centre.

All the kids at Grace House have a little saying, and end their day: "Goodbye teacher. See you tomorrow. Good luck for you! Good dreams for me!" Nobody remembers how the saying got started, but it is precious seeing the kids saying it, and makes me so proud of how hard these kids are working to find a path out of poverty!

Siem Reap, 2017 – The New Teacher

Grace House Community Centre is a vibrant, successful, ten-year-old community centre and school, that services the three local villages in the very poor area just outside Siem Reap, Cambodia. My daughter and I volunteered here six years prior, and I was back to volunteer for three months.

After a month volunteering, teaching English with adorable pre-schoolers and first graders, I was moved to the equally cute second graders. Their ages ranged from six to nine years old. Many poor families do not send their kids to school or preschool at the age most Western kids start school. It is unfortunate because these kids start to lag behind the others when they do enter school.

It is not unusual to have a kid two-feet taller and several years older in the same class as the age-appropriate kids. The reasons for the parents not enrolling the kids in school ranges from transportation problems of getting the kids to school, to using older siblings to look after younger siblings, and keeping them home when their peers are in school.

As I was teaching the adorable second graders one day, a smart, scrappy, usually dusty, seven-year-old Tong, raised his little hand and waved it anxiously. He asked the teacher in Khmer, the local Cambodian language, "How old is the new teacher?" The beautiful, 20-year-old teacher sheepishly translated and told me that I didn't have to answer if I didn't want to.

"Oh, no. I'm happy to answer," I said and held up a lot of fingers and said, "I am 58 years old."

Little Tong had a very puzzled look on his face and asked his teacher, "Is that the same as 18?"

The answer is, "Hell, yes!" it is, and until Tong learns to count to 58, I am officially 18!

Siem Reap, 2017 – Life in Cambodia

Cambodia is the 13th poorest country in the world. 114 other countries surveyed, have a higher GDP (Gross National Product) than Cambodia. It ranks poorer than Pakistan, Bangladesh, Kenya, Ghana, India, Nicaragua and Vietnam among others. It ranks slightly wealthier only to Zambia, Myanmar, Kyrgyzstan, Tanzania, Uzbekistan, Yemen, Ethiopia, Haiti, Tajikistan, Uganda and Mozambique. The poorest of the 127 countries surveyed is the DRC (Democratic of Congo).

Modern day life in Cambodia is difficult at best. Low wages, poor healthcare, underperforming and overcrowded school system, few career prospects, inadequate housing, poor infrastructure and no mass transit, are among the many social and economic issues. These all contribute to life's daily struggles for a Cambodian.

97% of the population of Cambodia are Buddhists, with Islam, Christianity and the local religion of Animism making up the other 3%. Since the 5th century, Theravada Buddhism has existed in Cambodia. It became the state religion in the 13th century. The exception is during the Khmer Rouge period in the 1970–1980s.

The village life in Cambodia is essentially the same as 100 years ago for many Cambodians. Many villages do not have electricity, phones or mail service. Few towns or villages have more than 5,000 people in them. Many roads are rutted and difficult to travel on. Only 14% of villages have a marketplace, 16% have health clinics and 33% have toilets.

The homes of the poorest people are constructed with bamboo, a wooden frame and a thatched roof. They are generally raised on stilts to protect from annual floods. The kitchen area is located below the structure. Homes of wealthier families are constructed with cement, tile and brick or masonry.

Many poor people sleep on the floor or hammock beds. Wealthier people may have a TV, sometimes running off of a car battery. Possessions are few; a few pots and pans, an oil lamp, mosquito net, straw mat and water containers.

Most Cambodians are rice farmers and are sustenance farming for their family's food. Owning chickens, a pig, a water buffalo or cow is a luxury and that family would be considered well-off.

Siem Reap, 2018 – Little Darat

I returned to Grace House six years after my first volunteer experience in Cambodia. I was there to volunteer teaching English and help out doing whatever I could for three months. I was so impressed with the wonderful example Grace House is as a non-profit community centre. The centre continues to help kids and families in the poorest socio-economic group in Cambodia, helping to make their lives better than prior generations. I was delighted to see that six of my former students were now teachers at the school.

It is a wonderful success story that these former students have graduated from the local university, or are attending college part time and are dedicated to helping out their community. I am so proud of these wonderful young ladies and their commitment, hard work, tenacity and sense of duty to Grace House. Private donations have helped these young ladies pay for their college expenses.

I was privileged to be able to spend three months volunteering, teaching English and being a part of the community. I believe the former students, who are now teachers, feel a deep sense of gratitude to Grace House for the opportunity they have been given to attend college. I have observed that they feel an obligation to the centre. They feel pride in returning the gift that they have been given, even though other teaching jobs pay a higher wage.

My second-grade class consisted of about 14 kids in the morning session, and another 14 in the afternoon. As hot, dusty, humid and bug-filled as our open-air classroom was, I loved every minute of teaching the kids.

These are kids that do not find it unusual for the teacher to have to chase the chickens, dogs, cats, spiders, mice, birds out of the room on a regular basis. I called these kids my toothless wonders! There is a high likelihood that the total number of teeth of all the kids would equal an adults' tooth count.

I was secretly chuckling as I would watch them try to eat the school supplied apple pieces for snack. It took an inordinate amount of time for the kids to finish eating on apple day! I am not a teacher by trade, but I did earn a TEFL (Teaching English as a Foreign Language) certificate, as well as 12 years' experience of volunteer teaching English. I also happily help out the teachers or staff when they want to practice or improve their English.

After spending a few months with the same group of kids and getting to know their unique personalities, I have developed my own observations. I felt I could pick out the 'Most likely to succeed' kids and what I felt were the 'Least likely to succeed' kids. Darat was on that second list.

Darat is a small, wiry, extremely active kid who goes into deep rebellion if he doesn't like what he is being told to do. The teacher and I tried to spend a bit more time with him, praise him for doing good work and give him a few projects to make him feel important.

Upon hearing about his very difficult home life, I decided to sponsor Darat. The amount of money it takes to sponsor a kid in need is insignificant in most of our lives, but makes a tremendous difference in the life of a kid in need.

I was told that eight-year-old Darat's parents both had abandoned him and left him with an elderly grandmother. She was also saddled with another one of her son's eight-year-old child, who I also taught. The second boy, Narin, seemed to be a much better, well behaved student. He also lived with the same grandmother, but had a father that was involved in his life and who gave money to granny to pay for the child's expenses.

I was told that granny withheld love, attention and care from Darat because she didn't get money from his parents for raising him. Darat was generally wearing the same dirty clothes all week, had untended cuts, was underweight and definitely had behavioural issues.

The wonderful social worker at Grace House, quietly, started to give sponsorship money to Darat's grandmother for his care. Sponsoring a child in need usually goes on anonymously, so as not to embarrass the family or make them feel indebted to anyone.

Four weeks later, as I was in my last week at Grace House, the teacher and I observed a significant change in Darat's behaviour. I noticed when the reward of a sticker or balloon was offered up; he was finishing his work first in the class. I was surprised to see the accuracy and care that he took in getting his work done. He happily handed out workbooks to the other kids, listened intently, stopped disrupting the class and stopped 'monkeying around'. He happily dove into his assignments. This was not the same unruly kid that I had just spent two months with.

The Grace House social worker followed up on Darat's home life and saw that he was indeed getting treated much better at home. This also was reflected in his school performance. I was wrong! Darat was now not on my 'Least Likely to Succeed' list, but on my 'Most Likely to Succeed list'. I will happily be paying for Darat to go to college, instead of bailing him out of jail!

One of my favourite photos of Darat was on a kickball day, as he decided the goalie cone would be a great hat. Another was of 22-year-old volunteer, Alex, lifting him over the five-foot barbed wire fence near the soccer field to chase down the stray 89 cent kickball!

Siem Reap, 2011 – Alex Volunteering

In Tucson, Arizona, fifteen-year-old Alex was quite experienced for her age at volunteering with kids and homeless folks. During a summer break, we were on our way to volunteer and teach English to underprivileged kids in Siem Reap, Cambodia. Two months prior to leaving, we talked about doing a fundraiser for the underprivileged kids. We came up with a slogan, 'Clothe a Cambodian kid for $15'.

We knew that $15 would buy some clothing, but we were not sure of the exact details. The thought was to give money that directly helped out kids and could be quantified into the number of kids you were helping, based on your donation. We put together colourful fliers and 'old school' mailed them to the list of friends and family.

The response was unbelievable and almost everybody made a contribution. We were thrilled, and Alex's fundraiser made $5,800. That was almost 400 kids we could help out. Alex meticulously wrote thank you notes as the money came in. I have found that acknowledgement and appreciation of donation money go a long way in securing future donations. She also did a follow-up thank you card of the happy, smiling kids.

Armed with donation money, we started volunteering at Grace House Community Centre, teaching English and an assortment other projects and areas that needed help. I was so proud of Alex as she spent the blistering hot, humid days assisting the preschool teacher with the gaggle of little kids.

She was also recruited to help teach the 20-25 'Adult Learners' who assembled for an hour, late each afternoon, to improve their English. I was never so proud of her, seeing her writing on the blackboard, explaining sentence construction and calling on students twice her age for the correct answer.

On our first day, we had a meeting with the head of the centre and several staff to explain that Alex had done a fundraiser and they are the recipients of the $5,800 donation. I observed the head of the centre about falling off his chair, as this 15-year-old pretty American girl told him of the gift. We explained how she raised the money and that the priority was to get the kids' clothing.

Dani, the wonderful local, early 20s social worker had a brilliant idea. We could employ a local non-profit women's sewing centre to sew uniforms for each of the roughly 300 kids. She explained to us that our village kids, and all Cambodian kids, can only attend the state sponsored school if they have a uniform.

Many of the kids in the extremely poor village of the community centre did not have money for uniforms. Some of these were kids from families of 5-10 kids per household. A uniform for each kid proved to be out of reach economically. That meant those kids could not attend local state school in the village.

Wow! Alex realised that the impact of her fundraiser far exceeded buying some kids clothes. Dani immediately started measuring and recording each of the kids' sizes, with a little wiggle room to grow. The sewing school was immediately hired and the project was off and running! We were able to visit the sewing school, sponsored by a French owned local hotel.

The sewing school had about 20 young ladies about 18-22 years old. We were told that they were illiterate and uneducated, and from small villages around Cambodia. This one and a half year long tailoring school would train the young ladies free of cost, and return them to their villages with a very marketable skill. This independence gave the young ladies a significant chance to improve their lives. The sewing school was delighted to have the assignment to make the uniforms.

Three weeks later, 300 uniforms showed up and Dani made sure each kid's new uniform fit. The kids were adorable in their white tops and navy-blue shorts or skirts. They were all so proud to have the new uniform. We took great photos, as we wanted to share the success with our contributors back home.

Alex was hanging with the other 15 volunteers in our lodging and seemed to make friends easily. We were all placed in different schools, but would see each other quickly in the mornings and at the end of the day and weekends. Nobody seemed to ask Alex how old she was, nor did they care, and they welcomed her into their group.

Off hour weekends were filled with beer, eating and clubbing. The group was off for an evening of night market and dancing. The other volunteers seemed to protect her, so I told them, "Just make sure she's safe!" It wasn't until many years later that she told me of her fun 'clubbing in Cambodia' stories! And her name as well as her friends' names, are still on the wall of the most popular club on Pub Street, Angkor What?"

Siem Reap, 2011 – Grace House Community Centre

As a mum of a 15-year-old Alex, I wanted to expand upon her knowledge of less fortunate people. She had been exposed to many local volunteer situations since handing out candy canes to the less fortunate folks in Tucson, Arizona. She had been doing this from age three, while sitting in her stroller. The rest of us gave out toiletries, books, snacks and helped the homeless make cell phone calls to their loved ones. Giving back time, money and simple compassion was part of my effort with my kids, to help them become better, more empathetic young people. Often our friends and school families went on volunteer adventures with us.

I decided to take Alex to Siem Reap, Cambodia, for a month to help work with underprivileged kids and expose her to travel on the other side of the world. Literally and figuratively, she taught four to five-year olds some basic English and had a huge following of admirers when she taught and encouraged the older girls to play volleyball.

Previously, it had been a 'boys only' sport and the girls stood shyly on the side, envious of the fun the boys were having. The tentative new female volleyball recruits giggled, missed balls, fell down, and at times got frustrated. But a week later, there was an increasing pride in their growing abilities.

They were having a blast, and more girls started coming to volleyball practice. Four weeks later the girls transformed into the most confident, happy, competitive girls the school had ever seen. And they almost beat the boys in competition!

It didn't even matter who won, they were out there having a great time!

Six years later upon my return, one of the teenage students recalled how volunteer Alex taught all the girls volleyball. I was thrilled to hear his recollection of this!

Siem Reap, 2011 – The Blind Massage

One of the most fun and entertaining parts of volunteering is exploring new, different and exotic cultures. I find the medium to larger cities much more vibrant and exciting than the smaller, quiet villages. One of our favourite things to explore after volunteering all day, are the night markets. The markets come alive in the evenings with every conceivable food, clothing, trinket, gimmick, gift, massages, restaurants, music and plenty more.

Many of the night market vendors work jobs all day, then at nightfall, they tend to their clothing and trinket booths, food carts, vegetable stands, hair salons and temporary food stalls. The Cambodian people are extremely hard working, gentle and respectful.

One market in Siem Reap had a building off to the side, offering massages by blind masseuses for $5 an hour. It sounded like a new, interesting experience, and the price was good. The feeling of supporting the blind masseuses made it sound even better. Alex, and 20-year-old British, Emily, and I were all set. We were led into a dark room with three massage tables in it, and were instructed to take our clothes off and relax face down on the tables, with a sarong covering us.

They told us it would be a few minutes to summon the two additional masseuses needed. "No problem," I said, and was happy to be relaxing on the massage table. We were each quietly in our own thoughts when five minutes later I felt hands on me starting to massage my back. This felt good! Then out of nowhere, the person forcefully grabbed my butt cheeks. I jumped up and shrieked! How dare they, I thought.

As I turned around to scold the masseuse, I saw Alex howling with laughter. She said, "I really got you good on that one!' Even the masseuse in the room was laughing! Not sure I've ever told anyone this story!

Siem Reap, 2011 – Alex's House

With the success of 15-year-old volunteer Alex's fundraising campaign in the USA, 300 kids at Grace House now had new school uniforms. Each of the students seemed to take great pride in their clean, white shirts and navy-blue skirts or shorts. Surprisingly, there was money left from Alex's donation. The Grace House staff met and decided that the village badly needed three additional water wells.

We were told that up to 10 families shared most water wells, and many of those families had to travel some distance to get the water. At $160 per well, it enabled the 10 current families sharing a well to reduce their waiting and walking time to get clean water faster and closer to their homes. The wells were quickly installed and resulted in many happy villagers.

It was also important to purchase a supply of medicine and hygiene supplies, as most families cannot afford either. We also wanted to make sure the kids had medicine, toiletries, sports balls and some basic sports equipment. After a tally of all that had been purchased, there was still about $2,000 left over.

We asked the Grace House staff for ideas as to what they felt was the greatest need in the area. The next day a proposal was made to us to build a Battered Women and Children's Safe House on the school grounds. There was at that time, no option or place for a battered woman to bring her children to escape a violent environment. "Absolutely!" we said. Digging began two days later.

Four weeks later upon returning home from Cambodia, an email came with a photo of a small wooden, two room house, with a roof of palm leaves. There were bright-pink curtains and two pink hammocks inside, as well as a sign on the front door that read 'ALEX'S HOUSE'.

Siem Reap, 2017 – Buddhism in Cambodia

Buddhism has been the state religion in Cambodia since the 13th century (with the exception of the Khmer Rouge period). It is estimated to be the religion of 97% of Cambodians. Buddhist monks are highly revered and are called upon to perform a number of functions in Cambodian life.

They participate in marriages, funerals, festivals, infant naming, ceremonies of rites of passage and many more life events. The monks' major function is to say prayers of blessings. They are still, and were often, also healers and in the traditional Khmer culture, and serve a role similar to a psychiatrist.

The monks are considered a living role model of good and meritorious living and provide their villagers with access to gaining merit, or good graces in the religion. Historically, they were the only literate members of a village. That is far less common now. Most of the Cambodian festivals are intertwined with Buddhist observances.

Many Cambodians are deeply superstitious and believe that through the monks and temples, they can give offerings to the temple to help keep evil away. Monks that are fortune-tellers and astrologers are important to Cambodian life. They are often consulted and advise on specific dates to marry, name children and report on what the coming year will bring.

Buddhists see the world as continually changing and life is a part of that continual change. They believe a person is continually born and reborn, in both human and non-human form, based on their actions of a former life.

The belief is that they are released from this life and reach Nirvana, which is achieved in this life through good karma. Good karma is achieved through earning merit and following a good path of living set out by Buddha.

Earning merit is important and can be achieved by giving money, labour or goods to the temple. Also, by providing one of the two meals a day, that the monks eat.

Children can earn merit by helping to look after fruit trees inside the monks' residence, or Wat. Young boys can become novice monks for a time of generally a year or less.

The young male, child monks have very often only taken vows of a few months during their school breaks. It is believed by the families that this offering of their child as a monk will bring good merit to the family.

One such belief is that the discipline and routine of the monk's life will also help their child mature, learn basic meditation practices, and become more polite. In small villages and remote areas, parents look to the monastery to provide an education to their young boys. At the age of 20, they can become a full monk.

Some young boys become monks if their parents have passed away. There are 227 rules that the monks must follow including times of eating and praying. There is also a rule that they may not sleep on too comfortable of a mattress. They may not dance, watch movies, handle money or participate in politics. In the early mornings, the monks walk the streets for people to give alms. The local people give them food and gifts in return for the monks' blessings.

There are over 100 temples in Siem Reap, which were built by a succession of Khmer Kings between the 9th and 13th century. Angkor Wat is the most famous of those.

Angkor Wat, which means Temple City, or City of Temples, is the largest religious monument in the world. It sits on a site of 402 acres (1,626,000 sq. metres). It was built as a Hindu temple for the god Visna.

It was transformed into a Buddhist temple by the 13th century. Its architecture is considered the height of classical style architecture and its likeness is represented on the Cambodian flag. It was designated a UNESCO World heritage site in 1992. Fifty percent of all visitors to Cambodia come to Angkor Wat.

It is said that a celestial plan was used in the placement and planning of the building of Angkor Wat. It is believed to be constructed by sandstone blocks and laterite. The binding agent for the blocks is unidentified and believed to be a type of indigenous resin. Most of the money to restore Angkor Wat is from foreign aid, and only 28% of ticket sale money goes into the preservation of the temples.

Over 5.6 million people visit Angkor Wat annually. In 2017 ticket prices for Angkor Wat topped $108 million, a 12% increase in revenue over the prior year. The streets of Siem Reap are overrun with buses of Chinese tourists as it is the fastest growing group of tourists to Cambodia.

Hundreds of new hotels have been built since my last visit to Siem Reap six years ago. China sent 1.2 million people to visit Cambodia in 2017. That was up 43% from 2016. It was 21% of the total annual visitors to Cambodia. Many of the restaurant signs are in Mandarin, catering to the Chinese clientele.

Angkor Wat is absolutely breath-taking at sunrise and is enormous is its physical layout. It is one of the most interesting historical sites I have ever seen. My favourite way to see Angkor Wat is by bicycle over several days. Definitely, worth a visit!

Siem Reap, 2011 – Teacher 'Good Job!'

As 15-year-old Alex was busy teaching the little kids, I had 28 eager 16-17-year-olds wanting to learn English. Grace House Community Centre in Siem Reap, Cambodia is a wonderful example of a non-profit school and community centre that works! Run by highly professional people, the positive impact it makes on the nearby villages is tremendous! Its theory is, "By helping the entire community, you can make a huge difference, and get families out of poverty!"

Roughly, 300 kids are taught English, computer skills, math, science, sports, art and reading, among other subjects. It supplements the half-day state school that is provided for Cambodian kids. The child can go to a state school if the family can purchase a school uniform and school supplies.

Knowing that new clothing was an issue with the kids, Alex did a fundraiser at home in the USA prior to going to Cambodia. Through the enormous generosity of family, friends and businesses, she raised $5800, which provided uniforms for each kid. This enabled all the kids of Grace House to be able to attend state school.

Six years later, upon my next volunteering experience at Grace House, there is still a high priority of supplying kids' uniforms and school supplies to ensure that they are able to attend state school, enabling them to continue their education.

I loved teaching my high school age kids English, as they were so eager to learn everything they could in English about the outside world. They were dazzled with computer pictures of other parts of the world and were mesmerised with photos of Hong Kong, pandas and snow.

Most of my students have never been outside of a 10-mile radius of their home village. Many of the village families are farmers and may have a small rice or vegetable field in which they farm, to feed their families. If possible, they sell their extra produce at a local market. Most families do not have a car or motorbike. Some of the kids come to school on an older, dusty bicycle.

Many have siblings on the back and front handlebars of their bike. None of the students had ever been on an airplane or big boat, or any exotic mode of transportation. Also, many of the teachers had not ventured far from the village.

The villagers lead very simple agrarian lives. According to Focus Economics, Cambodia is 13th of the 126 countries reviewed as the poorest countries in the world. This is based on the GDP (Gross Domestic Product) per capita. That is one of the bottom 10% of the poorest countries in the world. The average family income is less than $1,268 per year. As highly respected, revered and admired as teachers are, they can often make only $6 per day.

As the weeks progressed, I was so impressed with the students' work, dedication and enthusiasm. With my red marker, I would grade their papers and draw smiley faces, stars, hearts for the girls, and soccer balls for the boys. I would accompany their good work with a 'Good Job!' or 'Well Done!' on the top of the page.

I started to see some of the older, teenage boys smiling and soon laughing. I knew something was up, but I was not sure what it was. By the end of my volunteer teaching month, I just had to know what I was saying, that was so hilarious. I quietly asked one of the bright, attentive girls and she spilled the beans.

Apparently, when I was saying 'Good Job!' it was a little too close phonetically in Khmer to 'Ass Job!' I was mortified, and I am quite sure I was remembered as 'Teacher Ass Job!'

Siem Reap, 2011 – Weddings and Funerals

In Cambodia, in the Buddhist religion, a child that is not a normal child and is burdened with a physical or mental disability, or is gay, is considered to be living a life in punishment for the sins of a past life. Most families accept the misfortune and feel sorry for what they view as the afflicted person.

One such 12-year-old boy in Cambodia was a member of the village, where fifteen-year-old Alex and I were volunteering, teaching English. His name was Fa and he was a dirty, scruffy, small, bony kid for a 12-year-old. Fa had a difficult home life where the parents were not around to raise him.

It appeared that Grandma was in charge of him. Fa occasionally attended his second-grade class, as he was far behind in learning from his peers. His teacher told me he was disruptive and very difficult to have in class. I noticed Fa's sporadic attendance.

When I asked if he was mentally retarded, one of the local teachers told us that the villagers believed he was an evil manifestation of a bad spirit, and the villagers paid little attention to him. This was a college educated teacher telling me of this superstition. I felt so bad for Fa, but not quite sure what I could do to help him.

The teacher went on to say that Fa attends every local funeral and tries to attend all weddings. This is not because of his concern or caring about the deceased person, or wedding couple. It is for the free access to alcohol. His habit is that he attends these events and drinks alcohol to oblivion. That explained his school absences for days at a time, as weddings and funerals in Cambodia go on for several days. It was almost as if the locals were afraid of talking to, or confronting Fa.

As I as biking the four miles (six kilometres) to school the next day, I looked inside of the most recent funeral celebration, in it's all white, yellow and black silk fabric wrappings. There I saw a young boy who looked just like Fa. I never saw him after that and I hope for his sake that he is in a much happier place now!

Siem Reap, 2011 – Rice Bags

In Cambodia, there is no such thing as government supplied 'social security' for the elderly. Having many kids to take care of the elderly parents, has served as the family planning model for many centuries. In 1960, a Cambodian woman averaged 5.7 kids, as compared to 2.4 kids in 2016.

It is rare for an elderly man or woman in the village to not have a family to take care of them, but it does happen. Grace House Community Centre leads by example as the best community help program, I have ever volunteered with. They not only teach English to the 300 kids a day, they also take great efforts to take care of all the communities' members.

One such effort is the monthly distribution of large bags of rice to the single, elderly that do not have a means of support. I was lucky enough to get to go on a rice delivery day.

These are elderly folks that live in raised bamboo huts with palm leaves for roofing, to keep out the rain. I had never witnessed such sparseness of living conditions in my life. There were no kitchens or toilets in the huts. A small couple of bricks and a piece of wood or coal served as their cooking area, which was usually located downstairs, sitting on a dirt floor.

There was no running water or toilet in sight. We were greeted by each of the smiling, often toothless elderly in their frail condition. I think the human contact for them, was equally as important as the generous bag of rice. I didn't ask, but I don't think other food was plentiful. My heart went out to these folks. What incredibly difficult lives they must lead. I felt a huge sense of gratitude and was forever humbled by being able to visit the village elderly on rice bag distribution day!

Siem Reap, 2011 And 2018 – The Water Blessing

One of the most important elements in each village is its local temple. There is an enormous respect for the monks in the temple, as they are crucial in the daily lives and welfare of the villagers. While deeply superstitious, the locals use the services of the monks for many areas in their lives. Birth blessings, marriages, funerals, spiritual and astrological guidance and sometimes like a modern-day psychiatrist.

One such blessing is the 'Water Blessing'. Hindu in origin, it is a soul purification and guard against evil. Most of the locals I was acquainted with, seemed to get the water blessing about once a month.

Ten of our volunteer friends and I jumped on our bikes and headed toward the temple for our first water blessing. It sounded like a good idea, as the temperature was over 90 degrees (32 degrees C). Not knowing what to expect, but keeping an open mind, we shuffled to the raised platform of the temple in our modest clothing and sarongs.

Sitting down in front of the 30-year-old monk, we tucked our feet underneath us while our feet pointed to the back of the temple. Buddhists believe that the feet are the unclean part of the body and should never be pointing toward the altar.

The monk then had us come closer to him and he tied a red string band on our arm, as we placed money donations into a basket at his side. Monks are not allowed to touch money. He was continually chanting and praying the entire time. We then took a seat outside on a concrete set of stairs with our hands in a praying position. Minutes later, he scooped up a bucket of cool water and proceeded to drench us with our water blessing.

All the time chanting and praying, he continued for what seemed like 10 minutes, dumping water on all of our heads. It was cool water and there were a few initial shrieks, but it did feel good. As the drenched 10 of us cycled back to school, we all started laughing. It was a really unique experience!

I was also lucky enough to get another water blessing while teaching English in January 2018, and the experience was equally wonderful!

Siem Reap, Battambang, 2017-2018 – The Phare Circus

The Phare Circus is a group of young, highly skilled and trained performers that perform a 90-minute circus spectacle. It is a combination of circus arts, dance, music, comedy, acrobatics and movement which tell Cambodian stories. They perform traditional folk tales as well as modern stories.

The performers are from economically and socially challenged backgrounds and study and train for three years in the town of Battambang, Cambodia, before becoming an official circus member, performing in Siem Reap. The Phare Circus also runs a charity to help vulnerable children and adults in the Cambodian society.

The group was formed in 1994 by nine young men who came home from a refugee camp after the Khmer Rouge regime. The men were helped by an art teacher using drawing classes as therapy. The teacher wanted to help the socially deprived and troubled youth in Battambang, Cambodia.

They founded an art school and a free public school. A music school and art school were added next, then a circus school. Today, there are 1,200 students at the public school and 500 students at the alternative school. There is also an extensive outreach program. 'Phare, the Cambodian Circus' offers these students and graduates a way to earn a decent wage and teaches life skills. This money will take them out of poverty and give them self-respect and freedom.

Their performances hypnotise their audience with their emotion, enthusiasm and energy. I was fortunate to see three different performances and each had a different theme for the night. The audience of 300 people was happy, amazed and captivated by the skills and fast paced speed of the show.

Trip Advisor and Lonely Planet ranks the Phare Circus as the #1 show in Siem Reap. It is a really fun night and the performers are extremely gracious and will pose for many, many photos after their performance.

Indonesia

Bali, Ginyar, 2018 – The Little Kids

Nearby Ubud, I spent a month teaching English to a huge assortment of kindergarten kids and elementary school kids in both the Indonesian state school system and the smaller local kindergartens. The kids were wonderful, active, playful, mischievous and very fun to spend time with. Unlike my Thailand and Cambodian volunteering experiences, these kids did not appear to be in the same realm of poverty that I had recently experienced. Nobody was what I would call 'privileged', they just had more resources than my previous kids.

I was told that the government is a big believer in starting kids' education in kindergarten and it funds many of the programs adequately. Each kid had an adorable uniform of a solid bottom and a lovely local, brightly coloured batik top. The batik patterns were bright and vibrant and varied from school to school. There were lots of braids on the girls' heads, topped off by pretty colourful satin bows.

These kids had some resources in the classrooms. There were desks, white boards, notebooks available, some learning books and tools and a bit of artwork supplies. For the majority of the kids, it was their first exposure to English, both spoken and written. I use music, balls, bubbles, puppets, games, sports and other physical activities to teach the kids English.

We usually start a class off with a 'Dance Party', which by definition is some loud, popular music, and one or more kid dancing. It quickly becomes their favourite part of the class. I am legendary for my 'Dance Parties'. I keep a rotating playlist of everybody's favourite songs which is continually being added to.

If the kids are shy and don't feel like dancing in front of their peers, I turn it into a conga line of the whole class as we walk around the school while waving arms and legs.

Unbeknownst to the kids, they are quickly memorizing their favourite songs in English. I've heard many kids humming their favourite songs while doing other tasks. I throw in some other 'world music' from Spain, Africa, France and South America to keep their hearing sharp and to expose them to fun music from around the world.

I also use music in the 'before school', play programs and as a reward for work well done. It's also effective as after school fun, at sports practice and to wake up a sluggish afternoon classes. Very few people have ever fallen asleep in my English class.

I have had far more success teaching English when I make it fun. I like to reward good work and challenge the kids to succeed at their interests. I agree that sentences need to be dissected, 'past perfect tense' needs to be understood, and English tests need to be taken, but I like to think I bring a bit of magic to the classroom. There are many times that four consecutive balls are flying around the room while the kid holding the ball has to tell the class their favourite food, colour, animal or what they did over the weekend. The kids love the excitement of throwing the ball around to each other.

My favourite such list was the list of the eight-year-old Balinese kids. 'My favourite activity' was the question. The sweet, demure first girl raised her hand and said, "Going to the temple."

"Good job," I said. The list grew including cooking, playing football, reading, volleyball, sewing, dancing, Facebook, drawing and all the normal activities kids like to do. Little Kampee raised his hand and said, "Playing with a shotgun!"

"OK," I replied and proceeded to write 'playing with a shotgun' on the board. I had to turn toward the board because I was laughing so hard, I could hardly contain myself. Note to self… 'Remind me not to babysit Kampee!'

A week later, with adorable six-year-olds we were playing the game and throwing the ball around the class. 'My favourite food is…' was the topic for the kids. I started writing on the board all their answers that included, rice, papaya, chicken, coconut, satay. When I turned around, little Dong was wildly waving his hand. "My favourite food is Dog," pronounced Dong.

"OK," I said as I wrote it on the board. Looking around the class, nobody seemed to be as mortified as I was. So, I'm also probably not going to go to Dong's house for dinner anytime soon!

The best part of the Balinese kindergartners is the smiles and many, many hugs they reward you with at the end of class. That is my reward! Recess is always a blast, chasing happy kids as they run, hide, skip, jump and skin their knees. I find the poor kids, orphans and other less privileged kids equally as happy, enthusiastic and eager to learn as any child I've ever experienced in a privileged environment. In my experience, 'kids are kids!'

Bali, Ubud, 2018 – Beautiful Ubud

Ubud, Bali, in central Bali, referred to in books as the 'Arts and Cultural Centre' of the island. It has about 30,000 people in the town. It is a beautiful, exotic, lush, tropical area. It is also located amongst the numerous rice fields and steep ravines, dense forests and famous rice terraces of the central foothills of Gianyar. There are 13 villages that surround Ubud and each has a unique character to it. The area was originally important as a source of plants and medicines. Its name derives from the word Ubud, or medicine.

Ubud is also filled with a number of Hindu temples including Pure Desa, which is the main large temple in the centre of town. The economy is highly reliant on tourism. It focuses on shopping, restaurants, yoga studios, art galleries, boutiques, resorts, museums and zoos.

Ubud is famous for its Monkey Forest in an animal park in the southern part of town. Over many years, I have observed the thousands of monkeys getting increasingly aggressive in their search for food. Thousands of tourists have shrieked as the confident monkeys jump onto the head or shoulders of an unsuspecting tourist. Usually after the surprise of the intruder, several photos are taken with the friendly monkey on the tourists' shoulder.

As a designer, I find Ubud a treasure chest of craftsmanship and unique design. I love to wander the streets and discover the mostly small, boutique shops filled with wood carvings, original one-of-a-kind batiks, beautiful jewellery and creative clothing. There are spice shops, handicrafts, art galleries, lighting stores, paper shops, and jewellery stores.

Another treasure, is the absurdly cheap Bali massage spas. The standard rate is six dollars an hour for a traditional massage, or an hour long luxurious facial for the same price. There is a vibrant, lively restaurant and bar scene serving local and international food and cocktails.

Organic, hip coffee shops are abundant as well as numerous vegan and organic lunch and dinner restaurants. Ubud is a 'yoga paradise' with hundreds of practicing yoga studios. Ubud is also home to many local medicine men and chakra healers. Many ex-pats and international people choose to live in Ubud due to its charm, creative vibe, friendly locals, reasonable living costs and the beautiful surroundings of rice fields and natural beauty.

Bali, Ubud, 2018 – My Bali Big Kids

One of my favourite parts of volunteering is spending time with the other volunteers. That is, when there are other volunteers. Unfortunately, in many of the schools and orphanages I have volunteered at, I am often the only volunteer. I have no problem holding my own in a room or school full of people that speak a different language than I do. But it is always more fun to have the camaraderie of other volunteers.

Volunteers are generally 'like-minded' and seem to make friends, share in the triumphs, confusion, hard work, stresses, frustrations and failures of being in a foreign country trying their best to help out.

I am used to being stared at, whispered about, laughed at and generally the amusement of all. I understand it is usually because I look so different to them. I try to just keep smiling and carry on. Eventually, they get used to my presence.

I had the unique pleasure of volunteering teaching English and spending time with what I referred to as my volunteer 'Bali Big Kids'. Anna, Kate, Mon, Luisa, Sam, Ginny, Chloe, Siobhan, Saara, Beta, Sophie, Dorcas, Ashley, Courtney, Henri, Patri, Julie, Scotty, JM, Caetano, Kush, Sagar, George, Patri and John among others. These Bali Big Kids are all unbelievably smart, nice, empathetic, hardworking, educated, idealistic and full of life and adventure. Never once did I see any of them turn down a drink at the bar!

The common denominator of the Bali Big Kids is their desire to spend their precious time and money to volunteer and help out kids, animals or the community. These were not young people volunteering, just so they could list the experience on a resume, or to help their chances of getting into the college of their choice. These are young people truly interested in volunteering for all the right reasons.

The range of volunteering was from teaching underprivileged kids English, health, hygiene, sports, music and dance, math and games, to working on construction projects and animal welfare. Each volunteer had a unique story as to how and why they were in Bali volunteering. Each had a huge heart and a willingness to do whatever task was needed. Nobody was afraid of hard work!

I found out, through their stories that most were at a transition in their lives and wanted to do something constructive with their time and money. These are young people who are very intelligent, educated, kind and empathetic. Most are millennials who don't just talk about changing the world, they actually are making a contribution.

The construction volunteers would come back at the end of the day covered in dirt, sweat and mud after digging septic ditches for the day to help build new toilets for the schools and communities that needed them. The 'turtle' volunteers stayed on a quiet, remote island and cared for and raised endangered turtles to safety.

As volunteer English teachers, we needed extreme flexibility in school placements, lessons and teaching skills. We had a variety of kids parading in and out of the classrooms. One day a class would have 23 kids, the next day six would show up. Many a teaching day was complete chaos! We taught grammar, math, writing skills, reading as well as lots of hangman and word games.

Most volunteers committed to a month of volunteerism. I feel that is a good amount of time to accomplish goals. Less than two weeks teaching is difficult for kids to get an emotional attachment to a volunteer. I do understand it is difficult for most volunteers to take that amount of time off from the irregular life, but those that do find it immensely rewarding.

Most of the craziness generally happened off volunteer hours and usually with lots of alcohol involved! It was also lots of fun traveling with my Bali Big Kids to remote beautiful beaches, tops of mountains and insane nightclubs. There were motorbike adventures, sketchy bars, boat trips, a football match, rooster fighting, local celebrations and many, many, more crazy adventures.

The travel stories are fantastic. Holding one of the volunteer's hair up while she was puking in the toilet was not uncommon! As I have always said, as two of us were holding one of the wobbly girls up, "We have all been the girl in the middle." Talking a girl down from those last few shots was a regular occurrence. Somehow the responsible volunteer emerged early each morning, ready for the day!

On the next weekend, ten of my Bali Big Kids and I went to a super crazy, gigantic, hot, sweaty nightclub in Kuta, Bali. The large banner outside claimed it is the 70th best nightclub in the world. I'm going to go with, "OK," which will save me from having to visit the other 69.

An Australian guy about my age, with plenty of tattoos showing from his Bintang beer tank top, tried his best to chat with me, above the *Unce Unce* of the EDM music. My girls were at the bar getting drinks. After a few minutes, he asked if I had kids. "Oh, yeah," I said. "I'm here with ten of them." The guy ran away so fast I think there was a trail of dust behind him. It was back to policing my Bali Kids!

Many of the volunteers were continuing to travel all over the world after their volunteer experience in Bali. It has been great fun to see them all carry on with their interesting lives. I am still on social media with volunteers from 10 years ago and have followed their marriages, kids and divorces. How lucky I am to have such great people in my life.

Bali, Gianyar, 2018 – The Cock Fight

I pride myself on being non-judgemental, and for keeping an open mind. When my millennial volunteer buddies, Scotty and Sagar, asked if anyone wanted to go to the cockfighting event after volunteering that day, I was in. I seemed to be the only female that was curious to go see roosters kill one another. How bad can it be? And I figured I'd learn something about local customs.

Trusty local, Dewa, ushered us into a medium size dirty, dusty, simple arena that seemed to have about 400 excited men shouting and screaming. I quickly assessed that I was the only female among the group that was not selling snacks. Scotty, Sagar and I were also the only non-locals. I am very comfortable and have become accustomed to being the only non-local. I found this slice of life quite a fascinating experience.

I am guessing that almost every husband there had told their wife, they were hard at work all day. I saw crumpled up wads of local currency flying back and forth through the air. Apparently, that is the system the bookies use to make bets and payoffs. Some things in life, like gambling, seem to be universal. Not exactly high tech, but it seemed to work. Dewa explained the process of the cock fight.

As I understood it, the bird owners intentionally make their birds aggressive, wire a razor blade to one of the bird's foot, and let them fight it out until one dies. Clearly, all the shouting and yelling is the excitement of the people betting. As one bird dies, the crowd yells in excitement or lament, and the wadded-up money flies around the arena. Off to the side, groups of elderly locals were playing some kind of other gambling game. This was all serious business.

Lots of noise and activity was going on in the side show of gambling games too. My assessment of the cockfighting was, that it was not too much different from any gambling sport or casino. Just not as glamorous. I walked over to a small fire where a man was cooking and selling some kind of meat on a stick.

After grabbing handfuls of the mystery meat and handing them out to my buddies, we continued to watch the show. Scotty was throwing money to the bookie. I felt like we were really getting a sense of the local flavour. We were all having a good time. That is until a few hours later when Scotty turned pale, headed to the toilet and got terribly sick from the unidentified 'mystery meat' on the stick that I had given him. Or, whatever was on that stick! The rest of us escaped relatively unscathed!

Bali, Gianyar, 2018 – The Football Match

Volunteers Anna, Saara, Beta and I were teaching five- and six-year-olds English at a kindergarten located just adjacent to the large concrete stadium, that is the home of Bali United, the local professional football (soccer) team.

There were huge numbers of people, flags, merchandise and much excitement coming from outside the stadium. We asked Yani, our great local driver what was going on. "Big game today against Vietnam," he said.

"Wow! Can we go later after we finish with the kids?" I asked.

"Sure!" he said. We rounded up six volunteers and we were off to the big football match.

We had tickets in, what in the USA, we would call, the 'end zone'. It was full of young men and boys in their black T-shirts, head dresses, flags and banners. It was also quite similar to our USA 'student section' at college football games. The crown of about 4,000 was excited, loud and dedicated to their hometown football team. Apparently, this section of the stadium stands up and doesn't ever sit down for the entire game. This is so unlike my long history of USA football spectating.

My first observation was that nobody was drinking beer. We explained to Dewa, our local guide and driver, that this was highly unusual and that in the USA and Europe, beer was a staple at most sporting events. We then noticed two German travellers and their guide drinking what looked like beer, only it was in a clear plastic bag. Dewa quickly asked if we wanted him to get us some. "Hell yeah!" we all said in unison. Bali was playing tough, but behind.

Dewa showed up with several bags of beer. We all agreed this was our first bag of beer, ever. The locals looked at us with horrifying faces.

This was neither lady-like nor proper in their culture. We really didn't care what they thought! It was hilarious watching our group, consisting of Dutch, Irish, American and Mexican girls holding a bag of beer in the air and drink, what closely resembled urine!

The simple explanation of the bags of beer, replacing bottles of beer, is so that unhappy fans did not throw beer bottles onto the playing field. I dare not clue them into a wonderful thing called a paper or plastic cup!

The football game was really fun and we screamed and yelled for the Bali team. Bali scored two goals in a row, held off Vietnam, and won, in a great, exciting game! I have always believed that sports are the great equalizer in society and bring people of all walks of life together. I look forward to my next bag of beer!

Bali, Gianyar, 2018 – Nyepi Day

Just outside of Ubud, I taught a group of sixth-grade Balinese kids in an after school English program for several weeks. It was an interesting time of the year in that the largest, most important festival of the year, was less than a month away. It is called Nyepi Day. In Bali, it is a day of silence and reflection. I was told it was the most important holiday of the year for the Balinese. Trip Advisor called it 'A festival like no other seen on the planet'. It celebrates the Hindu New Year and was on Sunday March 17, 2018.

It is the quietest day of the year when all the people on Bali, regardless of religion, abide by the island rule of quiet. All routine activities come to a halt. All roads are void of traffic, airports are closed and people do not step outside their houses. The locals spend months creating papier mache effigies called ogoh-ogoh, or what we called the monsters.

The festival starts several days prior to Nyepi Day, and continues for days after. There are colourful processions of people all throughout Bali, where elaborate purification ceremonies take place. On the Nyepi New Year's Eve, the Balinese start at their family temple. They bless the family temple and chase away the malevolent evil forces from their compound. They bang pots and pans, hit drums and other loud instruments in an attempt to keep the evil spirits away for the upcoming year.

These spirits are later manifested in the enormous papier mache monsters and paraded through the streets. The colourful monsters are made from bamboo, cloth, tinsel and Styrofoam, and papier mache. They symbolise negative elements or malevolent spirits in Hindu mythology.

On the eve of Nyepi Day, the skies are filled with loud fire crackers, bamboo canons, smoke and flames.

On Nyepi Day it is a strict, no travel, no fire, no electricity six am to six pm and no leaving your home. The airports are closed. Only emergency vehicles are allowed. As a hotel guest, I experienced this fascinating day of silence. Our hotel was shrouded in a large, dense netting, and food and beer were readily available. No one was allowed to leave the hotel.

My travel companions and I, at the hotel, seemed to take the day in stride. It was quite an experience. It was strange seeing the skies devoid of airplanes. It was completely silent on the roads without the barrage of motorbikes, taxis, cars and people.

The following day, the island was loud, noisy, congested and back to normal, even though many celebrations continued. I was lucky enough to witness not only the New Year's Eve parades and celebrations, but the parades of many monsters through the streets of Kuta, Seminyak and Ubud. The detail, size and artistry of the monsters was unlike anything I had ever seen before.

In a strange way, it could be compared to the USAs Rose Bowl parade of floats in Pasadena, California, that precedes the popular Rose Bowl football game. In Bali, I could see that in one area of Kuta beach over 20 monsters, at the end of their parade route, were parked on the sand on the beach and were being judged and scrupulously inspected by a team of elderly, traditionally costumed men.

Some of the monsters get paraded around their respective villages then burned at the cemeteries on New Year's Eve. The most beautiful of the monsters are often displayed in community centres for an additional few months and sometimes the monsters are purchased by museums or collectors.

Bali, Gianyar, 2018 – Holiday Kids

After a week of teaching the enthusiastic 12- and 13-year-olds, we were getting closer to the Nyepi Festival time. My class attendance was getting thinner as most of the boys had disappeared. I was reassured it wasn't my teaching skills, but a family duty for the young boys to spend time making the village monster for the Nyepi New Year's celebration.

The construction of the scary, treacherous, evil, Nyepi monster is a fierce contest and source of village pride in its production and presentation on New Year's Eve. Each village takes the construction of the Nyepi monster extremely seriously. Given the heightened competition, families look to primarily the men and boys to produce the best monster possible. While driving past the temples and villages, there will be half constructed monsters on view over the month ahead of Nyepi Day.

I was determined to keep the interest of the girls that were still left in my classes and have fun with games, puzzles, music, board games and their favourite game on the whiteboard, 'Hangman'. I updated the Dance Party playlist with their favourites and they happily sang, danced and moved to their favourite songs. What seemed to be an unstructured class, turned out to be a great learning platform. We did more speaking English, than writing tutorials.

The drawings and artwork the girls did was stunning in its attention to detail. One of my favourite classroom things to do is to have the kids sign their artwork, and I tape it up and display it for all to see. I have noticed that it seems to be a very Western thing to do as hardly any of my classrooms have displayed student artwork. I do understand that kids also like to bring artwork home.

I have found it helps me learn their names. "Great picture, Shanti," I'll say as I am carefully trying to remember her name! I call this the 'refrigerator art gallery effect'.

When the kids know their art will be shown to a group, there seems to be a much greater effort on the kids' part to do their best and complete their work. I also see a sense of pride in their work as I carefully tape up the masterpiece. The great majority of these kids do not have a refrigerator at home, as that is an unrealistic purchase in their world. Even the very small kids are delighted when their art work is displayed for all to see. I also like to tape up and display math, science, spelling and other school work.

I noticed a different combination of kids each day in my after-school program in Tampaksiring, Bali. Several days, some of the younger siblings were curious and stayed for the lessons in my class. This was their older sibling's class, but they were curious and participated completely on their own initiative.

Break time was always fun and the four classes of kids joined together for running, sports, hair braiding, dancing and laughing. My other co-volunteer teachers were teaching these kids health, hygiene and safety in addition to English. I felt the older kids knew that the better they can speak English, the greater chance they have a getting a job in tourism in their future. This would be mainly in the thriving tourist industry in Bali. Many of these kids' parents are primarily rice farmers.

As I walked through the local neighbourhood each morning, I passed 20–30 farmers, both men and women. They were on their way to their respective rice fields to harvest or weed their fields. Most were welding a large curved machete-looking-sickle. As I was the foreigner, I smiled waved and said, "Selamat Pagi!" Or good morning in the local spoken language, Bahasa. I generally received a smile, nod or a "Selmat Pagi" in return. My new rule was: When passing a local welding a large machete, always smile and say hi!

I was happy to help out volunteering in the 'after school program' with my great kids, but it was time to say good bye! The important Nyepi holiday was approaching and I would be starting with a new set of orphan kids in a few days. The kids gave all the volunteers hugs and thank you cards, and lovely drawings I always tell the kids, "I will be back, I just don't know when." There are always tears in my eyes as I leave great, happy, fun loving kids. I know they will be fine!

Bali, Gianyar, 2018 – The Rice Fields

With some extra hours to spare in the day between volunteering, I decided I definitely needed to take advantage of the beautiful rice fields I was living amongst.

I am an avid daily walker and couldn't wait to check out my new, exotic surroundings. I usually listen to podcasts or favourite playlists or new music. My neighbourhood for next month had very narrow roads. They were about the size of a normal single lane of a road and had a white line dividing up the small road. The cars are relatively small in Bali and the drivers excellently manoeuvre the roads in an unspoken, usually calm, dance.

Somehow there are few accidents. It is impossible to go very fast on these roads, as there are many twists and turns in the road. There is also a parade of chickens, dogs, lizards, water buffalo, motorbikes, bikes, cows and kids. The roads are also used to dry the newly harvested rice on big blue tarps. Somehow, it doesn't bother the farmers when everyone drives over the rice they have placed in the street. It's normal.

If I was going to be walking the neighbourhood for the next month, I decided I would smile, wave, say good morning in the local language and make some new acquaintances. As I started on my walking journey, I noticed an inordinate amount of elderly farm workers in the fields as well as walking down the street to and from home and the fields.

I noticed that they all carried a rather large, curved machete that they used in the fields to harvest rice. This reinforced my belief in being nice, cordial and saying good morning to each local I passed. My new mantra was, 'It is in your best interest to be nice to anyone carrying a machete!'

With our local volunteer coordinator, we were able to go into the rice fields one day for a rice field experience and to say,

"Hello" to the workers.

We asked if we could take their photos, and they seemed to be flattered that we thought they were so interesting. They asked me if I wanted to thrash the rice stalks. "Sure, I'll make the rice," I said. They all stood by and giggled as I beat the handfuls of long, green stalks against their homemade wooden contraption. As I thrashed, wheat-coloured rice kernels fell into the pile they had been working on. They continued to think this was very humorous. I could do this; I could be a rice farmer!

I kept thinking for the next month how lucky I was to be there, teaching English. It really reminds me daily of how fortunate my life is that I'm on the opposite side of the world having an incredible life experience. The vast majority of these locals have never been off the island of Bali. Most have ventured more than a few miles past their village. It was explained to us by the college educated driver of the group that, "When one leaves Bali, they always return." He had left to get a college education in England, but returned back to his village after he acquired his degree.

These Balinese are happy, family oriented, deeply religious people who are confused by our Western ways and wanderlust.

Bali, 2018 – The Dog

With my cuts, scrapes, bruises and swollen knees from my two motorbike crashes, I decided I still needed to travel the 48 miles (78km) a day to volunteer with my Bali orphans. With some bandages and lots of Ibuprofen, I realised I needed to take the treacherous motorbike journey to the orphanage very slowly each way.

I needed to be rested, alert and reactive to all the chaos in the winding, narrow, rubble-filled, traffic-jammed street of Bali. It wasn't my driving that was the issue; it was the constant parade of aggressive motorbike drivers, anxious taxi drivers and angry truck drivers. That was before the constant parade of Bali dogs, chickens, cows, water buffalo, grandmothers carrying religious offerings, grandfathers on bicycles, and an occasional toddler wandering in the road.

The strategy of staying on the side or shoulder of the road seemed to be the correct choice. That is until I realised the road side is filled with gravel, broken concrete and oncoming motorists who do not look before entering the lane. I was doomed, but travelled on.

On a particularly scenic part of the journey, there are beautiful green, lush rice fields, there are moments of visual bliss. How beautiful this island is! That moment is abruptly halted by the noisy intersection with the policeman blowing his whistle and yelling at motorists.

After a wonderful, hot, exhausting day with the orphans I was on my long ride back to my hotel. Going slowly, but also anxious to get back, I spotted a large, grey, short haired Bali dog, sitting in the curb. His eyes were closed. Oh, no, he's dead! I quickly zoomed by. My heart went out to poor, old grandpa dog.

The next day I also passed poor dead grandpa dog. I was sad, that he must not have had an owner to give him a proper burial. The island of Bali is populated by a tremendous number of dogs without owners. By the third day of passing him I was getting really aggravated. How could the village people just let him sit 'dead' in the curb and scare everyone? I wasn't sure I could do anything about the situation. I was just upset that nobody was doing anything with the dead dog.

On the fourth day of passing by that location at my regular time, he was gone! I was relieved to see that someone took responsibility and hopefully gave him a decent burial. But wait, I saw old grandpa dog trotting along the sidewalk close to his former spot. He was alive and still kicking! Apparently, the curb was his napping spot and he liked to nod off every day about the time I drove by!

Bali, Ubud, 2018 – Chakra Cleaning

In my quest to keep an open mind and experience as many local customs as possible, I stumbled upon a sign 'Chakra Cleaning'. I had never had my chakras cleaned, so I presumed it was probably dirty.

Chakras are 'various focal points in the body used in a variety of ancient meditation practices of the Hindu and Buddhist religions'.

I learned there are seven areas including the crown of the head, third eye, throat, heart, solar plexus, sacral, and root. Apparently, blocked energy in our chakras can lead to illness, prohibiting free flowing energy. I was a neophyte.

The chakra areas are:

1. The head chakra, or crown, is located at the top of the head. It is the highest chakra and represents our ability to be fully connected spiritually. It is connected with inner and outer beauty and is connected to our pure bliss.
2. The third eye chakra is located between the eyes. It deals with our ability to focus on and see the big picture. It is connected to our intuition, imagination, wisdom and the ability to make decisions and to think.
3. The throat chakra deals with our ability to communicate. It deals with our self-expression, feelings of the truth and communication.
4. The heart chakra is connected with our ability to love. It brings us love, joy and inner peace.
5. The solar plexuses chakra is the upper abdomen and stomach area. Its purpose is to deal with self-confidence, self-esteem and self-worth.
6. The sacral chakra is the lower abdomen, below the navel and two inches in. It is connected to our sense of abundance, well-being, sexuality and pleasure.
7. The root chakra is located in the base of the spine and tailbone area. It represents our foundation and feeling of being grounded. It is associated with survival issues such as food and money.

The cleaning or clearing of chakras is presumed to balance our body and our mind. It is believed to balance fears and emotions that we are holding on to, as well as help physical restrictions associated with problems and pain.

Well, I was game to get going on my one-hour chakra cleaning with the elderly Balinese medicine man in Ubud. Fully clothed, he had me lay on my back as he started to chant. I asked him, "Eyes closed or open?"

He said, "Up to me." Definitely closed. I relaxed into the traditional beautiful Batik sarong lying on the table. Good thing I had a few local beers before.

I was totally relaxed. He was speaking in the local Bahasa language and continued to move his hands lightly on me and chant for the rest of the hour. I'm quite certain I had a little nap. After the hour, he said in his broken English, "Not so bad. All clean. But sacral may act up tomorrow." He communicated that I could ask him any questions I may have. I wasn't sure what questions to even ask, and I wasn't exactly clear on what part of me was the sacral that may act up tomorrow.

Apparently, I was clean enough to leave. I bowed, paid him and reported to my ten eagerly awaiting volunteer friends, who were quite hammered at the nearby bar. I reported to them that I was not sure exactly how the chakra cleaning went, due to my low expectations, but maybe tomorrow I'll have a better feel for it.

Oh, yeah! Six am it was definitely chakra cleaning time as I raced to the toilet. I continued to race to the toilet again and again. Good God, how much could be in there? I did make it out the door eventually. Apparently, with a clean chakra!!!

Bali, 2018 – Singing to the Rice Fields

As I struggle daily to motorbike the 48 miles (78 km) to volunteer with my Bali orphans, occasionally there are moments of beauty and peace. I am in Bali, where there is some of the most beautiful, breath-taking, serene and scenic parts of the globe. It is hard to take notice when the traffic is some of the worst traffic I have ever experienced.

It's not just the congestion. It is the craziness of the narrow roads, many potholes, winding roads, gravel in the roads and oncoming traffic in the wrong lane. That is before the parade of chickens, dogs, cows, water buffalo, basket carrying grandmas, rice drying in the road, grandpas on rickety bikes and the occasional toddler roaming the streets. Oh, and if you are lucky, you won't get stopped by the police!

In one of those rare scenic moments of motorbiking, I started humming Sting's Fields of Gold song from the 'Ten

Summoner's Tales' album of 1993. It starts with 'You'll remember me as the west wind moves, upon the fields of barley'. Wait! I had to look that one up. Is it true that Sting wasn't singing about the fields of Bali? So, for 25 years I have been envisioning a young, hot, tan, shirtless Sting with his sarong tied around his waist, in a rice field in Bali singing away, about the fields of gold. Damn, that vision quickly evaporated! I am forever saddened.

And yes, I'm the same person that thought that Steven Tyler from the 80s band Aerosmith was singing 'Do the percolator', instead of 'Dude looks like a Lady' in his song from 1987 Dude (looks like a lady). Not sure exactly what the percolator is though!

Bali, Ubud, 2018 – The Bali Orphans

For eight weeks in Bali, I volunteered with a great group of kids at an orphanage far, far from the beautiful beaches, hotels, nightclubs, fine dining and Villas of Seminyak. This is a different world, where the overworked, underpaid staff are trying their best each day to get the kids fed, dressed in clean clothes, get them to school, do homework, and tackle all the other issues kids have on a daily basis.

Walking into a new volunteer placement on day one is quite terrifying! We certainly don't speak the same language, as one of my primary efforts is to teach the kids some conversation English.

I have a theory that has served me well throughout many years of volunteering and not speaking the local language. I believe a volunteer should learn a few basic pleasantries, like 'Good Morning, Good Afternoon, Please and Thank You!' I then advise learning to count to 20. Next is to learn the local animals in their language. Dog, cat, chicken, water buffalo, lizard, donkey, horse, cow, bird and the most important, monkey! I have had hundreds of international conversations with kids with these simple words and they always laugh when I make the animal noises!

This particular orphanage in Tabanon, Bali is quite remote, and doesn't get a lot of volunteers or visitors due to its distant location. My favourite way to start to get to know the kids is through music. I bring my Bluetooth speaker that has travelled the world with me for many years and has entertained thousands of underprivileged kids.

I create happy, fun, popular dance playlists that seem to get the kids laughing, playing, dancing and singing! We play games, twirling, jumping, hopping and silly dancing, in addition to freeze statue.

They all seem to find it hilarious that the big white lady can also 'silly dance!' I keep the playlist short, and filled with music from the USA, Mexico, Africa, France, and other countries. They quickly recognise their favourite songs, give them their own names and ask me to repeat their favourite songs daily! My observation of most all the orphanages and schools, that I have volunteered for, is that there is little to no music available to the kids.

I have discovered the kids love music, and often it's the first thing they say when I walk in the door. "Music, music!" I also turn on the music before teaching class, during breaks and after class. I also used YouTube for the after school English lessons many days. I play a game with the older kids, English only… I put on a YouTube song, then they can pick one. It certainly expands both of our music repertoires.

It is truly amazing how kids love and can communicate through music. It also broadens their knowledge and breadth of music as well as teaching me about what they like in music. It also exposes me to new artists. That doesn't mean I like the Korean Pop group BTS, but I respect that they do.

Bali, Ubud and Tabanan, 2018 – Orphans Head Count

As I was getting familiar with all the names of my fantastic Tabanan, Bali orphans, I was working on a head count. Twelve, thirteen, fourteen, fifteen. OK. Got it! One of my favourite ways to learn everybody's name is by having them write their name on their schoolwork, picture or project that they have just completed. I can then look at it and say, "Nice job, Ketut!"

I find the kids become more familiar and attentive by using their names repeatedly. Balinese culture and tradition are especially kind to all of us foreigners trying to learn their names. Culturally, the first-born child is named Wayan, Putu or Gede. The second born child is generally named Made, Kadek or Nengah. Third born child is Komang, or Nyoman. Fourth born, Ketut.

After the fourth born child, it is an absolute maze of confusion with a combination of all of the previous names. It can also become a nightmare for teachers, as they may have five or six Mades in a class. It does seem to work itself out when they use nicknames.

So, I have a high likelihood of remembering their names as I think of the birth order. But it creates a traffic jam in classrooms when there are four Komangs, three Ketuts and four Wayans. Generally, they figure out another part of their formal name to use. As a last resort, I have often just said, "Hey little buddy, here's how you fly a kite!"

I was getting very familiar with all the kids, laughing, playing, throwing balls, feeding the little ones, helping with homework, hugging kids and drying tears. I was rescuing the balls in the trees, and doing all the things a mum does. I soon noticed three of the kids not eating at meal time.

I performed my best pantomime and attempted to ask why those three kids also went across the street at the end of the day to another house that the orphanage used for staff. I also noticed the three didn't have beds in the orphanage. The mystery went on for a week. I continued to play, teach and do art work with all the kids. I definitely wanted to cut little Komang's hair that was constantly in his eyes.

Finally, I discovered that those three kids weren't orphans at all. They were neighbourhood kids that spent all their extra time hanging out with the orphans where it was lots of fun, and cool stuff was going on! I'm guessing their mum wouldn't have liked it if I had cut Komang's hair!

I still laughed when I saw them every day. I treated those three kids exactly like I treat all the kids, with love, hugs, and lots of dancing and laughing.

Bali, Tabanan, 2018 – The Bali Street Kids Project

In Denpasar, Bali there is an orphanage and group of kids called 'The Bali Street kids Project'. It is run by a wonderful, energetic, compassionate woman named Putu. She has her hands full, running three orphanage locations, and over 100 kids. As with most orphanages, there is never enough time, staff or money to relax. She is so compassionate about helping these kids. She told me that after the terrible earthquake in Nepal in 2015, she went to Nepal and helped out in over 12 orphanages. She is truly a woman to admire.

She decided that the greatest need and utilisation for me as a volunteer, was the orphanage in a town called Tabanan. Tabanan was a 48-mile (78km) round trip to my accommodation. I visited one day and was immediately in love with the 13 kids. No matter how far I had to travel, I would make it there to the kids each day. The two littlest boys were four years old and constantly in a tussle with each other. The eldest of the kids were two, 14-year-old boys. There was also sweet Sara, a disabled 10-year-old girl.

Though most every child in an orphanage has a heart-breaking story, Sara's is especially heart wrenching. Sara is the child of a Balinese young mother and an Australian father. Sara was born with severe mental and physical handicaps and was immediately dropped off at the orphanage by her young mother when she was a new-born.

Although, several of the children have a family member that may periodically visit the orphan, Sara has not had a visitor, or parent check on her in her 10 years. It is quite possible Sara will never walk or be able to speak. But she seems to be delighted, sitting in her makeshift wheelchair, moving her hands and arms to the music coming out of the speaker. The other kids are extremely kind to Sara and give her hugs and kisses throughout the day, and sit with her, talk to her and feed her.

Sara needs around the clock supervision as she is in diapers and cannot feed herself. She has her own designated caregiver, who rarely had time away from Sara, except to shower. We made sure Sara was close by in her wheelchair for lots of our ball games, art projects, dance parties, English lessons and squirt gun fights. She thrived on the noise and excitement of the other kids.

Each kid has a unique and usually sad arrival story and I generally do not ask questions as to how or when they arrived at the orphanage. We call it a 'need to know basis', as it has no bearing on the kids' current day existence.

Sometimes the two wonderful house mums shared a story with me in our best pantomime and google translate from Bahasa to English. Dora's story was one of those heart-breaking tales.

I didn't realise until six weeks into my two months stay, that the charming, shy, happy six-year-old Dora was the daughter of Wyan. Wyan seemed to be in her early 30s and was the paid caretaker of disabled Sara. I was told that Dora was the third child of Wyan. Two of her older children had both been placed in another orphanage many years ago. She had previously abandoned the two older children.

I was so surprised because not once, in eight weeks, did I ever see any physical contact between Dora and her mother, Wyan. I thought Dora was just one of the 13 orphans, with no apparent parents. By no means do I blame little six-year-old Dora, she seemed to get love and attention from the other two house mums as well as all the kids. But I was appalled at how Wyan completely disregarded her own daughter.

After my first few weeks there, the two house mums hinted that Wyan was unhappy and would probably be leaving her care-taking job at the orphanage. They were actually looking forward to her leaving, as they felt her work ethic was not good and she did the minimum effort required. The day came when she decided to leave. I witnessed Wyan walk directly out of the orphanage with her suitcase in hand, not once looking back.

Apparently, she did not tell Dora goodbye, or anyone else! And that was the last anyone saw of Wyan. I cannot believe I saw a mother abandoning her six-year-old child! As my heart broke for Dora, I turned to look at the house mums. There were no tears being shed. Life in the orphanage resumed to its noisy, chaotic, busy, messy normal.

The physical size of the orphanage was similar to a medium-sized house. It was at best, a semi-dilapidated structure with four bedrooms, two small bathrooms, an outside covered kitchen and a rickety old clothes washer. The grounds had a solid lockable security gate for safety at night. The 13 kids were divided among three bedrooms. One of the house mums had a small private room. The other house mum needed to be next to Sara throughout the night.

As the house was adequate, it was hardly acceptable by Western standards of upkeep and modernisation. Huge areas of mould covered the ceiling of the boys' bedroom. Most doors had holes throughout, the lighting was minimal and the electrical was aging and in poor shape. But the house mums did their best to keep things clean. One bathroom toilet didn't flush, everyone just put a bucket of water in the toilet after use.

I was told there was going to be a new home built for the kids in the next six months. It was sponsored by a French NGO (non-government organisation). Still I requested that the mould be addressed and removed, for the kids' safety. A house in this condition would not be given a permit for occupancy in the USA. The interior of the grounds housed a car, a motorbike and several lines of drying laundry. It was hardly meant to be a playground for 13 kids. But like everything else in an orphanage, you make due.

We spent the months learning English, playing sports, doing artwork, playing football, learning about hygiene, practicing math and lots of dancing and game playing. I felt more like a mum playing with her kids rather than an English teacher. I had so much fun spending time with the kids.

About once a week, another volunteer would come and visit and bring supplies to the kids, or just help out. Each volunteer brings a new excitement and way of doing things for the kids. I feel it helps develop the kids' skills and keep the kids busy and involved. I absolutely love these Tabanan kids!

Bali, Tabanan, 2018 – Kite and Marble Day

One of my favourite activities with the orphans was 'Kite Day'. None of the kids had ever flown a kite. I purchased a hand full of kites from a local store and the kids were quite intrigued with them. We had some good winds, and I showed the kids how to run and lift the kites in the air for take-off. Their kites would soon be soaring high in the sky. The look on each kid's face as they recognised that their kite was indeed up in the sky was priceless.

The kids at the orphanage had very few books, art supplies, toys, games and sports equipment compared to most kids. The few hula hoops and deflated balls they had were often locked up in the storage room. The house mums were trying to keep the grounds clear and uncluttered.

One day, I noticed the four older boys playing the old-fashioned game of marbles with about five large, glass marbles. They had devised a game of marbles with their own rules. It's always intriguing to see how resourceful the kids are with their games and activities. Many games are played with flip flop shoes substituting for balls. Rocks, stones, twigs and leaves have been used to play all kinds of games the kids make up.

I did my best to bring balls, bubbles, colouring books, art supplies, jump ropes, kites, silly putty, dress-up clothes and makeup and anything else I could buy at the local stores. It is also a bit self-serving in that it gives me projects to do with the kids. One eight-year-old boy, Komang, asked me each day for marbles. "Yes Komang, I will look everywhere at the stores and find you some marbles," I said.

On an island with thousands of shops hawking tourist trinkets, I could not find any marbles. I'm thinking that the last time I heard of anyone playing marbles was 40 years ago. Apparently, there was no demand for marbles, therefore, no supply. Each day Komang met me at the gate of the orphanage, looked at me with his big brown eyes and just said, "Marbles?"

It was terrible, day after day, telling him I couldn't find them. I even thought about sending an Amazon package of marbles to the orphanage, but mail rarely gets to the recipient in Bali. I must have checked over 30 stores and nobody even knew what marbles were. There seemed to be no translation in Bahasa, the local language. Finally, weeks after my sad, little Komang started asking for marbles, I spotted four bags high on at the shelf of the local department store.

The look on Komang's face was priceless the next day when I showed up with his marbles! You would have thought the kid just won the lottery! I was his hero! And just as I was ever so pleased with myself, standing in the play area of the orphanage, a ball came and knocked me in the head. Back to reality!

Bali, Tabanan, 2018 – Artwork Wall of Fame

A big activity with the orphan kids after throwing lots of balls around, was artwork time. Thank goodness for colouring and activity books and coloured pencils. 'Hours of fun', as I call it. Armed with a roll of clear tape and some dull kid scissors, I started putting the kids' artwork up on the wall of the orphanage. This was something very new to the kids.

They had not displayed their schoolwork or artwork like many Western families do in their homes. I also used it as a way to learn the kids' names, as I told them to always put their names on the top of their paper.

The kids were really good at colouring, drawing and painting. It was fun to begin to paper the orphanage wall with their art work treasures. The kids of all ages wanted to display their drawings. The big kids helped the little ones write their names on their precious artwork and helped me hang up the masterpieces. Competition became fierce, as to who had more drawings on the wall, and who's were highest on the wall.

The wall was quickly filling up, so we rounded the corner and began filling a 25' (eight metre) long wall. After about three weeks, we had created an incredible, bright, vibrant art display of everyone's fine art. The kids were so proud! It also livened up the formerly, drab wall areas and brought a feeling of life and excitement to the orphanage!

Bali, Tabanan, 2018 – Sports and Games

In my first week at the orphanage, playing catch with a tennis ball proved to be quite the challenge. Fortunately, a donor had left 50 used tennis ball for the kids to play with. I started with the little kids tossing the ball and having them catch it, and then showed them the best way to throw a ball for distance. Somehow, we all think we are born with the knowledge of playing catch. Not so! I had 13 kids who had rarely, if ever, thrown a ball. Week one was a disaster! But we persisted, and practiced and practiced.

Progress was being made by week three. The girls joined in and were outperforming the boys. In the local culture, usually boys play sports, and girls tend to household chores. The girls' new skills caused a bit of envy and created extra effort on the boys' part to surpass the girls. The kids did great and by the end of my eight weeks, each kid could accurately throw and catch like a baseball player!

Weekly football (soccer) afternoon at the park was a favourite of the kids! The first day I experienced it, I wasn't sure what was up, or how this worked. I just followed the kids. Unlike our Western kids, these kids don't have the opportunity to play in competitive sports leagues or teams.

There is no money for lessons, uniforms or coaches. There is definitely not transportation to get to an event. What the house mums had created was the best substitute they possibly could. A donor had provided red T-shirts with a local football team emblazoned on the front. Each kid proudly wore what they called their 'football jersey'. They tied on some sports shoes and jumped in the crowded car, headed toward a local park for football time.

I hesitantly waited for another team to show up, but quickly realised that football time was a chance for the kids to get away from the orphanage and run around the mowed, grassy field.

I joined in with the kids as they pummelled balls toward the makeshift goal area and the goalie. Just the two hours in the hot sun, music playing, a few water fights and everybody laughing was my new definition of football!

'Makeup Day' with the girls is always a fun activity that the girls, and sometimes the curious little boys, love! It always reaches a tipping point from softly applied dainty makeup to Halloween style overkill. The demurely made up 12-year-olds would soon grab additional lipsticks and eyeshadows for their own experimentation.

The activity is usually over when each girl looks like a self-inflicted, heavily made-up transvestite! I always make sure I have wet wipes to return the little princesses to their natural beauty.

'Nail Polish Day' is quite similar, in that we start with the older girls, transition to the house mums and continue with the little girls and boys. Polish remover is a must! The little boys seem particularly taken with their new painted finger or thumb. They look at it as artwork. This is usually a teachable moment on hand washing, nail care and cleanliness.

Bali, Tabanan, 2018 − Traditional Dancing

On a rainy afternoon at the orphanage, the kids were filled with their usual energy and excitement. They were cooped up in a small room and decided they were going to show me some of the traditional Balinese dances they had been learning and practicing hard at. The boys and girls proudly dressed in traditional costumes, which had been donated.

The girls wore beautiful, brightly coloured, patterned, batik slim skirts. Each had a bright orange, pink, yellow or green solid colour sash tied around their waist. They held gold tipped, vibrantly coloured fans and were in their bare feet. They looked beautiful.

The boys wrapped a more masculine traditional Balinese batik sarong around their waist. It had a very intricate fold in the front held together with their own belt. Some had the local head scarf expertly tied around their head. They all wore their existing sports T-shirt of their regular clothes. The best shirt was four-year-old Ketut's shirt which read, 'Tough as a Bali dog'.

The kids turned on the video on the TV of traditional Balinese dancing and performed a fantastic, accurate, graceful version of the dances. They performed three exquisite dances for me. What a treat, they were wonderful! When I asked them, who taught them the steps, they said, "We just figured it out ourselves." I was in awe. I was so proud of each kid and their ability to dedicate so many hours to learn their cultural dances on their own.

After eight weeks of helping and play mum and teacher to the kids, it was time for me to leave. The outpouring of beautiful cards, love letters and drawings the kids made for me was overwhelming. I love these kids and from the notes I was looking at, they loved me too! I also, told these kids I would be back, I just don't know when. I cried all the way home, even though I knew these kids would be fine!

Bali, 2018 – Motorbiking in Bali

As I have discovered, motorbiking in Bali is extremely dangerous! The daily traffic is unlike any other congestion I have ever experienced. And I lived in New York City for 20 years! My transportation options were limited in traveling to the orphan kids in Tabanon, a 48-mile round trip to my orphans each day. Motorbiking made the most sense.

No wonder they needed help at the orphanage. Few volunteers wanted to travel the almost four hours a day. Thank God for Google Maps and the app, Maps.me. As I perched my phone directions carefully in a visible spot in my backpack, strategically on my motorbike, I started to learn the streets and all the twists and turns of the journey. The narrow roads, potholes, lack of street signs and plethora of people and animals in the road made an almost 'video game' of the trip.

I now understand the concept of motorbiking between two cars going in opposite directions. I soon became one of those people I never understood in the USA, as they motorbiked between lanes of cars. Soon, I was following the motorbike in front of me, in the lane of the oncoming traffic. Apparently, that is quite normal motorbiking for Bali.

The side of the road shoulder, where the slower motorbikes were supposed to stay, it was filled with loose gravel, oncoming traffic, chickens, grandma with fruit on her head, trees with large roots and the occasional rice drying in the sun on blue tarps. I'm not sure it was much safer, just slower than the main lane. In one rough week, I had two motorbike accidents.

Lots of blood, scrapes, scratches and a particularly banged up knee. It was swollen to epic proportions and took about eight weeks to be able climb stairs with ease. Fortunately, I didn't break any bones, but I was a frequent visitor to the pharmacy for ibuprofen. The orphanage house mums were really sweet and applied a mixture of garlic and onion on my leg in order to reduce swelling. I smelled extra great that day!

As I was still able to somehow get my swollen leg on the motorbike, I decided after two motorbike accidents that I needed to slow it way down. My bad week continued as I stopped at a particularly treacherous intersection, rather than go through the red light. I was directed by a policeman to his police hut.

In his best English, he said that my front wheel was on the crosswalk, and how much money did I have to give him! I had read many stories of the Bali Police extorting money from Westerners. It was true. I attempted to explain to him that I volunteered with orphans and I had recently had two motorbike crashes. His empathy metre wasn't working that day, and after paying a $25 extortion fee, he let me continue. Jerk!

A day later, I was stopped again by a policeman just moments from my lodging. He didn't even tell me why he stopped me, but my 'bad week' story seemed to pull at his heart strings. He decided not to extort money from me. The week was looking up! As much as I love my Tabanan orphans, I was never so happy as to the last time I did the treacherous 48-mile (78km) journey!

Indonesia, 2018 – Child Adoption

The process for foreigners adopting a child from Bali is extremely strict! The requirements are very rigorous and include: the couple looking to adopt being married at least five years and be between the ages of 25–45. They have to be residents of Indonesia for at least two years, be childless or have another Indonesian child. Having a child from another country excludes the prospective parents.

The parents must be of the same religion as the child's biological family, and be able to appear in court. According to the USA's Department of State, 4,714 children from Indonesia were adopted in 2017. In contrast, in the USA, 271,831 children were adopted in that same period, both domestic and foreign.

I was fortunate to have witnessed the tight family bond of the Balinese people. Multi-generations of Balinese families live in the family compound. Each family compound also includes a family temple. The Balinese tradition is that when a girl of marrying age in the family marries, she goes to the husband's village and family compound to live. On a few rare occasions, I met some 30-year-old, working men, who were not from a nearby village, and did not live with extended family.

And even those young men believed that when they found a wife, they would return to their respective villages in distant islands to marry and raise their families. They had left their villages in an effort to find work, but always intended to return to the family compound.

When I asked a foreign educated Balinese man, why there aren't more Balinese immigrants living throughout the world, he told me, "We may leave Bali, but we will always return to our families, culture and home." He explained it is a religious and cultural way. That is also how they want to raise their children.

I did notice that of the many people I encountered in Bali, few had ever been off the island. I sensed no curiosity from any of them about seeing the world, or anything other than their own culture. Walking down the busy tourist streets, the shopkeepers are continually hustling, cajoling, and asking questions of the passer-by. "Where are you from?" is a common conversation starter. I find the shopkeepers could care less where a person is from, it's just a ploy to engage the person in conversation, and get the tourist to look at their wares for sale.

When I asked various locals if they had ever been on a plane, not one had. That can be an economic issue, as well as a lack of adventure issue. They will gladly tell you how many days it takes by boat to get to relatives and family on various islands. Many working young people try to go home once a year, to distant islands, to see their families and relatives and aging grandparents.

Fertility rates in Indonesia have dropped significantly from seven children per woman in 1960, to a current day 2.6 children per woman. I repeatedly heard from locals that 'kids are expensive', and that was the main reason for limiting their families.

Divorce rates in Indonesia have risen dramatically from 1999, with the numbers of divorces at 20,000 per year, to over 200,000 per year, 10 years later. The Balinese women have a greater awareness of their rights than previous generations, and are becoming more economically independent. They are refusing to put up with infidelity, abuse and domestic violence. Differences in religion can cause marital friction. There is a 90% divorce rate in Indonesia of couples with different religions.

Interestingly enough, I never saw a 'House for Sale' sign on a residence, in my extensive travel around Bali. While glancing at one of the few real estate offices in Ubud, the only residences I saw for sale were a few, new, single family homes for rent or sale, or a small hotel.

This is because the family compounds are passed on through the many generations. As the family grows, additional structures are built. It is not uncommon to see the construction and building of multi-level additions to the family compounds, as they are unable to build and encroach on their neighbours' compounds.

The family compounds have centuries old Hindu based influence. Each area of the compound has a particular orientation as to the location of the family temple, sleeping, cooking, socializing and bathroom areas. They pay particular interest to the directions of the sea and Mt Agung, the tallest mountain in Bali. They will refer to the area of the compound facing the ocean or facing the mountain. The direction east and west is referred to as 'where the sun rises and where the sun sets' as Bali is eight degrees south of the equator, and very close to exact east and west. Often three generations live in the family compound.

Bali, Ubud, 2018 – The Role of the Medicine Man

The Balinese have an ancient Hindu belief in Balian Taksu, or medicine men. There are four times as many of these medicine men on the island as there are doctors. There are roughly 8,000 medicine men helping over 4.5 million Balinese people. The Balinese believe they draw their power from spirits or from nature. Their medicine is derived from plants, holy water and flowers. Some medicine men will communicate with spirits and possibly go into a trance while healing people.

A traditional doctor may be called upon to treat certain tangible ailments, like broken bones or certain diseases, but when it comes to intangible illness, the medicine man healer is generally used. He will usually take a more holistic approach to the ailment than a medical doctor and consider mental stability, emotional issues as well as the physical issues in finding a cure for the ill.

For treatment, the patient is seen as willing participant in the healing journey and the treatment can include herbal potions, cleansing rituals, and possibly inscriptions drawn on the body. Balinese people are historically known as superstitious people, and will seek out a medicine man for advice on black magic and ill spirits, as well as emotional issues that manifest in physical illness. Holy water is commonly used to bless in the medicine man's practice.

I started visiting Bali in 2001. It was a year prior to the devastating, senseless 2002 terrorist bombing of a nightclub in Kuta, Bali. Reports claim 204 people were killed including the two suicide bombers. Locals claim over 500 people were killed.

Many people hurt in the tragedy, were locals and headed back to the irrespective villages for medical care and those that died were believed to be unrecognised in the fatality statistics. There is a 'Bali Bombing Memorial' at the site of the original 'Paddy's Pub', the bombing target. There is a plaque that identifies the 88 Australians, 38 Indonesians and people of more than 20 different nationalities that were killed that tragic day. It was a very sad chapter in the country's history.

Ubud, 2010-2018 – The House Liyer

I love Bali! I am enthralled by the culture, design, food, atmosphere, music, the kind and gentle people, as well as the natural beauty of the island. Apparently, six million other foreigners agree with my assessment and visit the island annually.

In 2006, Elizabeth Gilbert wrote a New York Times best-selling book called *Eat, Pray, Love*. It stayed on the New York Times best seller list for 187 weeks and sold over 10 million copies. The book wildly helped to popularise Bali as a tourist destination. In 2010, the movie *Eat, Pray, Love* opened, starring Julia Roberts and Javier Bardem. It depicted

Bali as a gorgeous, lush, tropical island of beauty and splendour.

The skies were cloudless, the rice fields immaculate, roads not congested. The houses were works of art, temples abundant, batiks vividly colourful, and the locals were perpetually smiling. Yes, some days are like that!

In her book, Ms Gilbert visits the local elderly medicine man, Ketut Liyer. There is some confusion on his part as to how old he is. "When I asked him his age, he said 96, 87, I don't know," said Ms Gilbert. Even today, on the outside of the house the sign reads, "Ketut Liyer–House and Family." Underneath on the sign it reads, "Medicine man, healing, meditation, palm reading, Balinese astrology, pain healer."

The House of Ketut Liyer became enormously popular, based on the book as well as the movie. For $25-$40 Ketut would spend up to 15 minutes with you and do a palm reading and chat, in his best attempt at English. I, too, was curious, as well as sceptical, as to what the great medicine man would say about my future! Armed with my best traditional batik sarong, modest T-shirt and traditional colourful sash, I was ready for my first visit in 2006.

After waiting an hour, and wandering the beautiful grounds of his family compound, it was my turn to talk to the great, ninth-generation healer, medicine man, Ketut. His family compound was filled with the sounds of hundreds of chirping birds from their cages, a vast collection of intricate wood carvings, lush exotic plants and flowers, and a family temple located in the far corner of the property. There was also an assortment of large TVs and leather sofas sprinkled in the various open, gathering areas.

Ketut stood up, greeted and smiled at me, with what seemed to be a three toothy grin. He laughed and said, "I have to pee."

"No problem," I replied, and sat in my best cross-legged half Buddha pose. Shortly, he returned with his irresistible, almost toothless smile. He laughed and held my left hand and asked what country I was from.

I honestly don't remember most of what he told me those many years ago, as I'm quite certain he forgot my information moments after the next person sat down. But I clearly remember him telling me I would have three marriages. Well, I kept that piece of information to myself, as I was in long-term relationship number two. I'm going to chalk Ketut's bit of information up to his elderly memory, maybe being, not being as sharp as it once was. My first visit to the great medicine man Ketut of Ubud, Bali was a fun, interesting few moments in a great trip!

As luck would have it, two years later, I was able to return to Bali for a holiday after volunteering for a month in the slums of India with my daughter, Alex. On this trip to Bali, I had nine millennial travel buddies. We were on a two-week Indonesian adventure. The travel company I used, specialised in local, sustainable, small group travel to parts undiscovered. They were not kidding! Most of our types of adventures rarely made it into the travel brochures. It was a real local, 'slice of life' trip, full of crazy adventures through Java, and Bali.

As the Indonesian trip was ending in Bali, I had mentioned to my new friends that I had gone to see the well-known medicine man, Ketut Liyer. They were keen to go visit him and learn their futures. We scheduled time for the group of us girls to go. The three guys were less excited, but would accompany us. The crowds at the House of Liyer had waned, from my initial visit, which was shortly after the initial popularity of the 2006 book *Eat, Pray, Love*. But Ketut's wisdom was still popular and sought out.

I watched as my travel buddies, each in their traditional sarongs, stared intently on Ketut. Each girl seemed to be shaking her head "yes" and asking several questions. They seemed to be enjoying their conversation with Ketut. He seemed to be doing most of the talking. As each girl finished, the rest of us were extremely curious as to the discussion and outcome of each visit. The girls were filled with information about their futures, all beginning with Ketut saying, "You are a very beautiful girl."

As we all finished, the most stunningly beautiful, Canadian girl of the group said, "He didn't tell me that!" We laughed and said, "That's because you already know you are beautiful!"

Again, I don't recall much of the conversation that Ketut and I had, but I do remember him telling me again, that I would have three marriages. OK, I'm going to call that coincidence. My happy travel buddies and I continued with our crazy adventures in Bali. We climbed mountains, visited temples, drank lots of semi-cold beer, hiked volcanoes, saw beautiful rice terraces, experienced the jungles and saw lots of monkeys. We decided visiting Ketut was a really unique, fun experience. We definitely had a story to tell our friends back home!

Well, this was the second time he told me about his prediction of my three marriages. Upon returning home and after some time, I told my two closest friends of Ketut's prediction. We all laughed and were convinced he must be wrong!

Several years passed, sadly Ketut Liyer died in June, 2016. He was reportedly 100 years old, but nobody, not even Ketut himself, was certain of his age, although he did remember that he was born on a Thursday. He was the ninth healer of succession in his family. He is succeeded by his only son, Nyoman Latra, as the 10th medicine man of the Liyer family. After his death, the writer Elizabeth Gilbert described Ketut, "He was a healer, a mystic, a time-traveller, a word bender, a mind-shaper, a compassion-expert, a flirt, a comedian, a bozo, a hustler, a magician, a trickster and a fully ascended spiritual master. On the morning he died, an earthquake rocked across Bali, as the earth said farewell to one of its great masterpieces. He will not be coming back to this world. His work is done." Elizabeth Gilbert once asked Ketut if he would like to come visit her in America. He shook his head and said, "Don't have enough teeth to travel on airplane." He was a wise, unique, happy, unforgettable man that I was privileged to have crossed paths with twice!

Recently, on a Christmas holiday break from university, my daughter, Alex, and I ended up in Bali. Alex was very familiar with Bali, as she had volunteered several times at a local orphanage in Denpasar, Bali. She looked forward to seeing and catching up with some of the now mature and grown-up orphans. She happily reported, they were doing well in their jobs and life. She also said, "Hey, Mum, let's go see the medicine man!"

We were off on motorbikes to Gianyar, outside of Ubud, in the chaotic, noisy, unpredictable traffic, to visit the House of Liyer. I had explained that we would be talking to Ketut's son Nyoman, and she said, "Great." She is 22 and few in her generation have a reference to the *Eat, Pray, Love,* book of 2006 or movie from 2010. She was open for any experience and was curious to ask him questions about her life, as a soon to be college graduate.

The grounds of the House of Liyer were extremely familiar, and brought back memories of my previous visits. Gone was the former line of people that midday, and we were quietly and happily ushered in. A family member took the suggested $25 donation per person, and he chuckled as I tried to correctly wrap my sarong in an acceptable manner. Apparently, my sarong wrapping wasn't to his satisfaction, and he continued to give me a tutorial on the correct procedure. He was laughing the whole time. OK, I do have other talents!

Wrapped in her traditional sarong and sash, a smiling Alex looked enthralled during her 20-minute chat with the current medicine man in the House of Liyer, Nyoman. She later told me of the many things he told her after looking at her left palm. She was excited and happy and said, "He told me I was beautiful and smart." I did not want to burst her bubble and reveal that like his dad, he too is a flirt, a showman, a teller of fortunes and a treasure of the community.

It was my turn. I explained I knew and respected his father. I'm sure he has heard that line thousands of times before. He happily grabbed my palm and talked of how I was healthy, would live a long time and was smart and beautiful. I laughed and told him he had eyesight problems, as I am old, and the beauty torch had long ago been passed to my daughter.

We had a fun chat and when he saw the side of my hand he said, "Three marriages!" Good God! I can't seem to get away from my fate. Well, I explained, I just ended number two, didn't marry him, but spent many years together.

"So?" I asked, "What do you think the timing is on number three?"

He smiled and laughed and said "Be patient."

I had two additional visits with Nyoman recently as I brought eight of my adorable, co-volunteer, millennial 'Bali Daughters' to see him.

There seemed to be a bit of resurgence in tourist traffic to the House of Liyer, and the girls anxiously awaited behind other world travellers. Much of the same information was exchanged about how smart, beautiful, healthy everyone is, and the bright future and long life ahead. But I could see as each girl sat with Nyoman, there were some deeper discussions.

Some of the girls criticised his repetitiveness. After hearing their concerns, I, as the elder of the group, enlightened their perspective. I told the girls that culturally, the Balinese young ladies their age, do not leave home, rarely travel, marry locally and young, rarely are given the opportunity for an education and often live in economically challenging situations.

So, I explained to the girls, to Nyoman, he sees a young 20-something year old girl, volunteering half way around the world, completed or completing an education, suntan from the weekend beach adventures, wrapped in a beautiful sarong with a flower in her hair. Yes, you are all beautiful, smart, and will live long, my lovely Bali Daughters! I'm also convinced Nyoman is the envy of many men!

The second of my recent visits to Nyoman, was with my best friends from the USA. Janell, my best friend forever, had heard the many stories over the years from me of the great House of Liyer. She was curious to go visit and see what stories Nyoman held for her. Janell, her sister Carol and beautiful 22-year-old Gretchen were all game to hear of their futures.

I, frankly, was running out of topics to talk to Nyoman about. I discussed my two recent motorbike crashes and how I was writing a book of my adventures to inspire people to volunteer. He told me to slow my life down, write my book and come back to Bali with a finished book, and he would bless it! How can I argue those words of wisdom?

As he's reminding me again to come back to him with a finished book, he points to a dusty, aged, stained frame holding the *Eat, Pray, Love* book cover. Oh, that was the book that sold over 10 million copies! "My father blessed her book," he said as we parted!

Bali, 2018 – Getting Exhausted

As much as I love my Bali orphans, the 48-mile (78km) motorbike ride every day was exhausting me, as it would be for anyone braving the absolutely insane craziness of Bali traffic. It is like no other traffic I have ever experienced in the world. The traffic jams, confusion, noise, heat, police, cars and massive numbers of motorbikes all contribute to the perfect storm of accidents. The rental, sub-par motorbikes, with their lack of decent brakes, speedometers and gas gauges that don't work, broken blinkers, cracked mirrors and more, help contribute to the danger of travel in Bali.

After motorbiking almost 240 miles (386 km) a week to get to my kids at the orphanage, I had two motorbike crashes in one week. No broken bones, but really banged up, with swollen knees, bruises, cuts and scrapes. It hurt like crazy, and many trips to the pharmacy for Ibuprofen and bandages were the new norm. I now know why most locals are bundled up in long sleeve jackets, pants and gloves even in the 90-degree (32 degrees C) weather. It's preventative crash gear!

To add to my misadventures, I also had my $1,600 iPhone stolen in Kuala Lumpur by a motorbike thief, while on a weekend visa renewal trip. That was a nightmare. I was also stopped twice by the Bali Police and it was highly suggested that I pay them off. I did pay one of them. My tears, and showing them photos of my orphans, did elicit some empathy on the second police officer. He also wanted to get rid of the foreign lady crying in his traffic hut, so he let me go without his usual extortion fee.

Add stomach problems and diarrhoea to my misadventures and exhaustion, and most people would have packed their backpack and headed home. I had promised myself I would continue, and finish my volunteer year, no matter how difficult it was. Giving up was not an option. I am very driven! So I powered through. I needed some time off to heal and get better and rested.

I needed to take a break, and be a tourist!

Bali, Ubud, 2018 – Cinderella

My best friends from the USA could not have come to Bali for a visit at a better time! I was exhausted, both physically as well as mentally. I had been volunteering and away from home for six months. As I hobbled to meet them at the Denpasar, Bali airport, I wanted to cry. I missed them so much.

Although I'm regularly on social media with my kids and friends, it was so nice to spend some great days catching up with them and filling in the blanks of everyone's life. After I had exposed them to a few days of local food and housing, they bumped it up to five-star beautiful hotels, and food. I had completely forgotten how that used to be my life. We pieced together both modest local adventures with five-star experiences and had a fantastic time.

A few months after their return home, I was Face Timing with them. They are extremely well-travelled. I asked them where they felt the Bali trip ranks on their travel experiences and they both said top or right near the top!

We all learned from the experiences and I can accurately say that a massage at a five-star hotel trumps my local $6 massage ladies! I was able to show them the best non-tourist parts of Bali; the breath-taking beaches, waterfalls, rice terraces, local markets, temples and many restaurants and bars.

A quick weekend trip to Phuket, Thailand to see another best friend was equally as wonderful. As I said my goodbyes to her from the stunning five-star resort, I passed the four beautiful swimming pools, the lush gardens, exotic dining spots and the gym. I slipped out the resort's back gate, to bargain with a ripe-smelling taxi driver, sleeping in his car and had just woken up, to take me to the airport. I truly felt like Cinderella's beautiful carriage had just turned back into a pumpkin!

Bali, Denpasar, 2013 – The Orphan Kids

I have often said that the most fun experiences us volunteers have with the kids in an orphanage, is to go outside the orphanage and have an adventure. The kids most often go from home to school and back in a monotonous cycle. The kids learn so much when they get outside and experience things most other kids take for granted.

The issue is that these adventures cost money, which is generally scarce, and can require additional staff to help. Transportation is also an issue, getting all the kids to the adventure location. I have heard many stories of very kind locals, who will take a car full of kids to a yoga or dance class, ceramics studio, swimming pool or sporting event.

One of my favourite events that we started with the kids was sunset on the beach in Kuta, Bali. We took the kids swimming in the ocean, and to a traditional Balinese cooked meal at a local restaurant. These kids were thrilled to have a soda and run around the beach before sunset, or just sit and talk. We also made sure we brought a soccer ball, for a lively informal game of soccer. Jumping up and down in the waves was another favourite, and we don't claim to have taught kids to swim, I just say we taught them how to 'not drown'.

After sunset, we would walk 15 minutes to the local restaurant and let the kids order what they wanted and dive into the food. We would talk a little about proper manners at a restaurant, and the kids learned quickly. These kids are extremely well-behaved, as they know if they act up, they will not get to go on the next trip.

I found, the two evenings a week we would do this adventure, enchanting. We would have to divide up the kids into two groups, so we could handle the trip better, and get to know each child. I would mix up the ages, and seat a volunteer at each table with kids. I saw that the experience was really special for the volunteers also. Sunset and dinner out, soon became everybody's favourite two nights of the week.

Bali, Denpasar, 2014 – The Orphans' Garden

We volunteers are given the task of everything from teaching English, helping with homework, doing laundry, wiping tears, playing games, teaching hygiene, reading books, listening to kids and what I call 'doing everything a mum does'. This is also with a kind heart and no judgement. This is one of many reasons I so admire volunteers. The majority of volunteers are doing this on their own time and money, while their contemporaries are having much more glamorous vacations.

My observation is that 90% of the volunteers I've worked with are female. I don't have a scientific or accurate reason for this. When that rare male volunteers, they are extraordinary people. Let's also say that they get an enormous amount of attention from the females! Take note, boys! My thoughts would be that a lot of volunteering with kids can be perceived as maternal.

I think it is so important for orphans to have a good 'male role model', as most of the staff are heavily female dominant. My heart melts when I see the male volunteers work with the kids on a project or learning experience. I've seen kids delighted while igniting the paper mache volcano, catch a ball, learn soccer moves, get chased around, or just hung upside down by a clowning male volunteer.

These young boys want a hero and a male figure to emulate. Although they have books containing super heroes, they are not certain of the qualities that make these guys so special.

As a volunteer, there is a thrill to finding an activity that is new to the kids. That's when the best conversations happen. I usually bring many bags of books, clothing, toiletries, games, sports equipment, reams of blank paper, school supplies and some toys.

One year, I decided to go to the local Home Depot in my hometown and buy lots of packets of seeds for flowers, fruits and vegetables. I wasn't sure of the exact growing climate, so I just bought a big assortment. I also brought gardening tools and many pairs of gardening gloves. We weren't sure where or how the garden would happen, but we could figure it out upon arrival.

We got lucky, and the orphanage had an existing, functional garden that was tired, weed choked and forgotten. Apparently, the worker in charge had abandoned it. Great teachable moment! we thought. We pulled weeds, tilled, hoed and prepared the medium-sized garden area.

We had taught the kids a few basics about gardening, and explained that a garden took time to grow, and had to be tended to. That it may take a month to see a result. But by the end of that week they could see small greenery sprouting. We explained the importance of watering, weeding and of caring for what we were going to plant. The kids were as dirty and tired as we were, but were having fun. The kids were planting the seeds very close together, but as the plants grew, we would show them how to separate and give the plants room for growth.

The infant vegetable, fruit and flower garden quickly started to grow, and the kids were amazed that they had created this. They fought over who got to water and weed the garden. By week two, it was sprouting and by week three we were thinning out the various vegetables and flowers.

By the end of the month, the kids were becoming quite the gardeners and we had a huge amount of flowers and the beginnings of vegetables and fruits. The experiment was a huge success and a great idea for future kids.

Lombok, Gili Trawangan, Bali, 2018 – The Earthquakes

An earthquake registering a 7.0 on the Richter scale, hit the Indonesian island of Lombok on August 5, 2018. Lombok is about 24 miles (39km) of water from the popular tourist destination of Bali. The death toll has been reported at over 430 people, and over 350,000 people have been displaced. Over 68,000 homes, businesses and mosques have been destroyed. Many people are sleeping in makeshift tents by the road, as safety precautions, from aftershocks. Experts predict the death toll will continue to rise, as bodies are pulled from the rubble.

As of August 14, 2018, Indonesia has been hit with seven earthquakes in the prior nine days. Dozens of small tremors and major aftershocks have hit the region in an area struggling to return to normal. Indonesia sits on what is called 'The Ring of Fire', in the Pacific Ocean. It is home to 90% of the world's earthquakes, as well as 81% of the world's largest earthquakes.

NASA and the California Institute of Technology have reported that the island of Lombok has risen 10 inches. They used satellite images to create a ground deformation map that measured changes in the island.

Hospitals are flooded with the injured. Food and water are desperately required, along with medicine and shelter for the locals. Crumbling roads have slowed efforts for rescue workers to reach the survivors. Many mosques and villages were completely destroyed.

I awoke early August 5th, in Legian, Bali. The bed and room were shaking for about 30 seconds. The clothes on a nearby hanger were rocking and swaying. Is this a crazy dream? After taking a few deep breaths, both the building, and I calmed down. I wasn't the only person, who opened their door and looked out, looking for some kind of answer or at least a connection that all was 'OK'. Very soon, all was back to normal. Back to sleep!

I was soon on a boat for my scheduled trip to Gili Trawangen. Other than a crazy boat journey with enormous waves, making the boat rock like I had never experienced, all seemed normal. The news reports of the earthquake damage from Lombok were starting to hit the media and they were devastating.

WI-FI is extremely slow and frustratingly hit or miss on the Gili Islands, so most people were not up to date on the incoming reports of the destruction on Lombok. Three days later, I was scheduled to leave and was told the small 'fast boats' could not make the normal, one-hour journey, across the water to Bali. We travellers were told we would 'small boat' it to Lombok, bus to the large ferry in the south of Lombok, then slowly make our way to the Bali port.

After a 16-hour journey that day, we were unaware that a second, almost as powerful earthquake as the August 5th one, had hit Lombok. 500 of us travellers were on the large ferry and were unaware of the earthquake. It was a taxi driver that filled me in on the news as I headed for an inland town, Ubud.

There were two more earthquakes in the following days where the room was shaking and windows rattling. The hotel owner said there were large waves in the swimming pool. It was such a strange experience. We travellers ran outside our rooms, away from the building structures.

News reports showed nearly 2,000 panicked, stranded travellers in Lombok and the Gili Islands, where I had just left. Apparently, I had just made the last boat off the island, before all boats were ordered to shut down, due to excessive waves. There was also some concern of a tsunami in the area. Many locals and travellers headed for the only hill on the island of Gili Trawangen, to feel safe. The tsunami warning was soon lifted.

I now understand the strange feeling of anticipating more earthquakes. I started to sleep in my clothes, with a clear path to the door.

My deepest sympathies go out to the victims and their families of the horrendous earthquake that continues to devastate Lombok.

Yogyakarta, 2010 – The Market and Granny

One of my favourite times of the day to explore while travelling, is in the very early morning, just after sunrise. It is, what I call, the 'shop opening' part of the day. I usually seek out the local food markets and regular markets in whatever town I'm visiting. I am always amazed at the vast numbers and varieties of things I have no idea what they are, or how to pronounce.

The streets look so different in the early morning, and take on far different characteristics during the busy, bustling, rest of the day. Early morning streets are usually filled with yesterday's garbage, dust, and remnants of the prior day's commerce. My favourite is the early morning opening and chaos of the food markets or bazaars. There seem to be an abundance of older people and people my age. Perhaps they too have the old person's sleep disruption problems that plagues myself and friends my age.

There seems to be a lot of head nodding and acknowledgement of the international 'Wake up early people'. I am convinced it also makes for a productive day with the early start. I am usually quite the oddity as I wander the aisles of the numerous markets filled with innumerable fragrances both exotic and putrid. There are displays of meat, fish, bread, vegetables, flowers, cleaning supplies and everything else imaginable.

I am clearly not a local. I'm just up wandering the aisles ungodly early and I don't look like I can cook the local dish. Most people just ignore me.

Often a walking street is used to sell market items, where there isn't a covered, specific market. I would call it, most similar, to one of our Western farmers' markets. Lots of hustle and bustle, people bargaining, weighing produce, spices, tea, meat.

On one such market street in Yogyakarta, on the island of Java, I saw a makeshift dental clinic on one of the open-air walking streets. Several elderly folks were seated in small plastic chairs howling with pain. A man in a white lab coat seemed to be playing the part of dentist, with a young woman frantically trying to help patients.

I swear I saw him using something that closely resembled a pair of pliers as he tugged and tugged at the exasperated patient. I said a quick, "Thank you God for Western medicine and dental practices." The dentist soon spotted me, freaked out and started waving his hands and yelling something to me in Indonesian about "getting the hell away!" Hey, I'm not the one holding pliers. I hurriedly passed the secret dental operation and continued down the street.

Yogyakarta, on the island of Java, is a city of over four million people. The island of Java is the world's most densely populated island in the world with 2,435 people per square mile (1,067 people per square km). 58% of Indonesia's population or roughly 151 million people live on the island of Java. Indonesia is the fourth most populated country in the world with over 261 million people. The point being that Java is crowded!

As I continue my early morning stroll through the open-air markets of Yogyakarta, I walked to the end of the bustling market, and went several more blocks. It was increasingly quieter the further down the road I went. Old, somewhat grimy, shabby homes cluttered the street. This is not a good or fancy part of town. Rusted sheet metal and old corrugated tin-roofs serve to keep rain out of the makeshift houses, shops and shelters. I always find these off the path areas the true realities of a city.

Getting away from the popular areas and into the real, gritty parts of the life of the city is where I find the real heart of a city, town or village. I had truly found that part of Yogyakarta.

I spotted a somewhat small, old, rusted, gated graveyard ahead. I completely respect the locals and respect their dead, but the streets were empty. I was curious to see what an Indonesian graveyard looked like. As I quietly moved closer, I wasn't exactly sure what I was seeing. Yes, the tombs, headstones and memorials seemed awfully close to each other. Moving closer, I honestly could not believe what I was seeing. It was a new, bright white, silk coffin sitting about four feet off the ground, abandoned and placed on top of another tomb.

Just when I thought the markets were extraordinary and unique, this was very strange. I carefully moved closer. Oh my God! The top of the casket was slightly open, about a foot, and ajar. I am not certain what the explanation is of leaving Granny in an open casket atop another tomb, but I am quite certain I will never witness that one again!

Bali, 2018 – Mt Batur Hike

One of the most interesting, and challenging things to do in Bali is to do a three am mountain hike to the summit of Mt Batur to catch the incredible sunrise over Mt Agung at 5,633 ft (1,717 metres). The lava filled slope of Mt Batur is about a two-hour hike to the top of the caldera, which last erupted in 1963.

Mt Agung, Bali's highest mountain and active volcano has erupted over five times since late November 2017, and most recently in July 2018.

When Mt Agung erupted, on November 27, 2017, over 100,000 people, from 22 nearby village evacuated their homes. Airports were closed for three days, and 400 airline flights were cancelled. This resulted in a decline of 30% in tourism for the 2017 holiday season in Bali. Starting in September 2017, the 10-mile radius of Mt Agung experienced 300-400 seismic earthquakes, causing seismologists much alarm. Evacuations started at that time, as the alert level was raised to its highest level. The height of the ash upon eruption, reached 1.5 miles (two km) above Mt Agung.

The atmospheric ash exposure was believed to affect over 5.5 million people in the densely populated surrounding areas. The Balinese believe that Mt Agung represents the central axis of the universe.

A few months later, with Mt Agung relatively quiet, it was a good opportunity to do the nearby Mt Batur hike. Six of us in our volunteer group signed up for the adventure, and definitely had second thoughts as the one thirty a.m. alarm went off.

Armed with halogen headlamps, we hiked with our guide up the gravelly, steep path to the top of the mountain. It was definitely, fairly straight up, with few switchbacks or level areas. After two hours, breathing heavily and covered in sweat, we had reached the summit of Mt Batur. It was still dark, but at least we got to sit and drink coffee and wait for the magical sunrise over beautiful Mt Agung.

Sunrise was not only stunning, but the feeling of accomplishment and awe overtook all of us. It was such an emotional moment. We weren't the only ones relishing in the beauty. I looked behind me and saw around 200 others who had also hiked the mountain. We all had the same big idea!

We were extremely careful when we reached the top of the mountain, as we had just heard a terrible story the night before. One of our volunteers, who is an Irish nursing student, had helped a young British girl, after she had a life-threatening fall into the caldera just days before. Many broken bones and internal injuries resulted from the fall and she was in a local hospital recovering.

We were extremely careful and decided to walk the loop of the caldera for another two-hour hike before heading down the mountain. It was a breathtakingly beautiful view. At times, slipping and sliding on a four-feet (1.3 metre) wide path was nerve racking because it was a steep, massive drop on each side.

We all finished intact, and happily hiked down to the base of the mountain. We all really enjoyed the experience and couldn't wait to tell our other volunteers to go for it! Just don't drink too much the night before.

Bali, 2010 – The Orphans and the Poster

At the orphanage in Denpasar, Bali, we five volunteers were getting very comfortable with the almost 50 kids. We were staying with them at the orphanage, so that meant seeing and helping them from sunrise until bedtime. One day, seventeen-year-old Alex and I took a large duffle bag of supplies that we had brought from our home, upstairs to the girls' room. Along with bringing school supplies, games, toiletries and workbooks, we often brought clothing from home that was in good shape. We always knew the kids needed the clothes far more than we did.

This particular day, we had about 12 girls politely gathered around us hoping for some handouts. They weren't sure what was in the bag, but it held promise. I started lifting piece by piece, asking the girls, "Who needs a blue skirt, pink T-shirt, pair of dress pants?" Very politely, each girl had several treasures as we made our way through the bag.

Eleven-year-old Meta quickly reached into the bag and pulled out something completely foreign to her. "OMG!" said Alex, "I left my tampon box in the bag." Meta was perplexed and opened the pink wrapper, started giggling and threw the other tampons at the girls.

"Mum," said Alex, "Go get the poster." She meant the large 4' wide x 3' high (1.3 x 1 metre) detailed drawing of a vagina and all its parts, that we had stumbled upon in the TV room days before.

I made a deal with her. "You go get the poster, and I'll give the talk," I said.

She handed me the rolled-up poster as I was rehearsing my speech in my head. "Ladies," I said "This is a vagina! We all have one." The girls looked at the massive vagina staring them in the face. The looks ranged from horror to terror!

"Oh, no!" I said, "It isn't this big." I scrambled and showed them my fist and said, "It's more like this big." I finally talked them down from their horror, and calmly finished my female anatomy talk. Everyone survived, and felt that they had earned their new clothing.

No way was I doing the sex talk with these girls! The next volunteer could tackle that one!

Nepal

Kathmandu, 2018 – The City

Kathmandu is a city of over five million people and is the largest city in Nepal. The country of Nepal has 29 million people and is the 48th most populated country of the list of 168. In land area, it is 93rd largest country. It sits at the base of the Himalayan mountains at 4,600 feet (1,402 metres) above sea level. Nepal has eight of the world's top 10 tallest mountains in the world. Mt Everest is the highest point on earth at 29,000 feet (8,848 metres) above sea level.

The Himalayan mountain range is spectacular. Tourism is the number one industry in Nepal, with over 940,000 tourists visiting each year. Over half the tourists come from India, China, US and the UK.

In April 2015, Nepal was devastated by 8.1 magnitude earthquake that killed over 9,000 people and injured 22,000 others. It left 3.5 million people homeless and entire villages were flattened. It is considered the worst natural disaster to strike the country since the 1934 earthquake in Nepal.

The 2015 earthquake affected Nepal, India, China and Bangladesh. The damage to the Nepalese economy was $10 billion, which is 50% of the Nepalese GDP (Gross Domestic Product). Tourism dropped 31% from the prior year.

The earthquake triggered an avalanche on Mt Everest, killing 21 people. That was the deadliest day ever on the mountain.

Nepal is 81% Hindu, 9% Buddhist and the balance a mixture of Islam, Christianity and other religions. Nepal has 36 holidays a year, which is the most number of public holidays of any country in the world.

In 2017, Nepal was in the bottom 8% of GDP per capita in the world, at $834 per person. It is a proud country, but incomes are low and poverty relatively high.

Pokhara, 2018 – Trekking the Annapurna Circuit

I arrived in Kathmandu, Nepal ready for a new adventure. I had never been to this country, and looked forward to all the unique culture, food and adventures it had to offer. I decided to go on a four-day trek called the Annapurna Circuit. It is one of the most popular treks, as there are hundreds of variations of trekking in the Himalayas from day hikes, to climbing Mt Everest.

In Nepal, a hike is considered a day trip. The Nepalese define trekking as a multi-day hike. It can sometimes be up to 20 days. Mountain climbing is altogether different, requiring special training and equipment. Mountain climbing also comes with far greater risks.

Nepal is famous for trekking due to its affordability, abundant lodges, trained guides and high safety record. Nepal also has eight of the highest 10 mountains in the world. Mt Everest being the highest mountain on earth at 29,000 feet above sea level (8,848 metres).

The main, income generating activity in the mountain region, is tourism. Hiring a guide and a porter means the trekking tourist is supporting a Nepalese worker and several families. It is also common to make friends with the guides and porters as a trekker spends many days with them. It is a great way to learn about the culture, festivals and even some local Nepalese language.

The use of a guide is invaluable in the case of bad weather, zero visibility, cold temperatures and permits. The most popular and diverse trekking area is the Annapurna region.

I chose a four-day trek, which was leaving from Kathmandu. I was by myself, and was happy to join a group of five 30–35-year-olds, very nice business professionals from Borneo.

They all spoke great English. Upon meeting them, they talked of how they vacation together and had climbed several mountains. They all had on expensive, new boots and outdoor clothing on and dragged huge suitcases for their two weeks of vacation from their professional jobs.

I was totally intimidated by my fancy new friends, and prayed that I could keep up with the enthusiastic group. What did I get myself into? I had just come from Bali and had a backpack of teacher clothes, sarongs, bathing suits and coconut oil.

We headed to one of the many trekking supply stores. I'm going to make a wild guess that all the clothes labelled with fancy brand names, were highly unlikely from 'said' manufacturers' stock. Most likely, good knock offs! I stocked up on hiking boots, a hat, a warm rain jacket, and trekking poles. I felt like I was a senior citizen with my trekking poles, but figured it was better to have them than not.

Early the next bright and sunny day, we headed up the rugged mountain. And I mean UP! I'm not sure there was anything flat or remotely like a switchback that day. I didn't want to lag behind the group, and again hoped I wouldn't embarrass myself due to lack of speed. But I was no stranger to exercise and walk miles and miles each day as my regular exercise. It was just that I had been at relative low altitude for a long time.

I started to notice that the group was actually going really slow, and each twist and turn provided them an opportunity to take more and more photos. It was also apparent on the guide's face that they were really slow. Who knew I'd be the speed demon of the group! The guide let me walk with a porter, who carries the tourist's bags, and we bounded up the mountain.

I found the quaint small villages, dotted all over the mountains, so fascinating. These mountain folks were highly self-sufficient with their small gardens, farm animals, small lodges and an occasional school. The lodging was clean and simple, often with the most magnificent views of the Himalayas out the window of the hotel room.

Packs of donkeys and horses, loaded with supplies and propane tanks were frequently passing, and occasionally other trekkers from all parts of the globe. The most spectacular sight, was a predawn two-mile (3.2km) hike from our lodging, up to the top of a mountain called Poon Hill. As the sun rose, our group along with about 30 others, was treated to the breath-taking sight of the sun hitting the eight highest mountains of the Himalayan range. Every five minutes, a new perspective of light and reflection hit the mountains. It was the most magnificent sunrise view I had ever seen.

The four days of trekking was such a great experience. I had been able to trek at my own pace, and make friends with four of the porters, who also acted as our guides. I learned all about their families, villages, kids, farm animals, beer they liked and girlfriends.

I tried my best to learn Nepalese, and the porters were extremely patient with me. My volunteer travel theory with kids is that you can have a conversation with any kid in the world if you can:

1.   Count to 20.
2.   Say 'Good Morning, Good Afternoon, Thank you'.
3.   Learn a bunch of farm animal names.
4.   Most importantly— 'Sit down and SHUT UP'.

My theory has been tested in well over 10 countries and has served me well. By the time I get to 'sit down and shut up', they think I know a lot more of their language that I actually do. And, they really do listen to me!

I highly recommend to anyone looking for a great adventure, to go trekking in Nepal.

Nepal, 2018 – The Devastating Earthquake of 2015

I asked many locals about the horrific Gorkha earthquake in November 2015. Over 9,000 people were killed and 22,000 were injured. It created $10 billion of damage, which is 50% of Nepal's GDP. It is considered the worst disaster in Nepalese history since the 1934 earthquake. It also triggered an avalanche on Mt Everest, killing 21 people, as well as killing 250 climbers on a nearby mountain. It was said by relief workers that the area looked as if it had been hit by a nuclear bomb.

Several of the people I met and talked to were from the area of Gorkha, which was the epicentre of the 8.1 Richter scale earthquake as was reported by the China Earthquake Networks Centre. The Gorkha region was the hardest hit area, with the largest casualties and most devastation. I heard stories of how most of the elderly family members died, because the quake was at noon when the elderly traditionally were inside their homes, taking a nap. One woman told me how she was in the village outside of her home with her baby and truly thought the world was ending. But they were OK.

Hundreds of thousands of Nepalese were made homeless and entire villages were destroyed. One of the UNESCO World Heritage sites in Kathmandu had many buildings that were destroyed. Aftershocks and landslides also contributed to the disaster.

There had been scientific warnings in 2013 predicting the sufficient energy accumulated in the underlying Nepal region to produce an 8-magnitude earthquake.

I was told stories of the massive destruction of the surrounding areas and how most all of the homes were destroyed due to the fact that they were made from earthen bricks, and had no steel structural elements.

Apparently, the government funded each family $3,000 for home repair, but the locals told me that was nowhere near enough to rebuild.

Disastrous events in very poor and politically paralysed nations like Nepal, generally have decades of strife and recovery. The after effects of the earthquake have had subsequent consequences on seemingly unrelated aspects such as human trafficking, labour costs, property cost burdens, mental health, disease, public debt, tourism, healthcare urbanisation and more.

A survey reported that 30 months after the earthquake, only 12% of the reconstruction money was distributed, and those without land were locked out of financial support. This created an exacerbated social divide, feeding on the poorest of the poor.

After several minutes of discussions about the devastating earthquake, many local people told me they would rather not discuss it any longer. Again, showing the resilience of the people, they just get on with their lives.

Pokhara, 2018 – The Fortune-Teller

After my paragliding accident, tumbling down the mountain on take-off, and breaking my leg, I was confined to a cast on my leg and crutches. It was my first broken bone in my life, and I didn't realise how difficult it is to manoeuvre with crutches.

After five weeks of recovery, I was able to hobble using only a walking stick. I was diligent and did many hours of daily strengthening exercises, and walked as far as possible. By the next week, I could walk, ever so slowly.

I was so fortunate to be in the lovely town of Pokhara, with its large lake and very pleasant lakeside walking path. For several days, I would pass a 60ish, traditionally dressed fortune-teller who was holding his book of mysteries! I would just smile and say, "Namaste!" as I would pass him.

After about four days, as I passed him, he mentioned in broken English, that his fortune-telling services were for hire. "How much?" I asked. He shouted out a number, and I was temporarily confused with my conversion rate. It was $20.

"Too much," I said.

"OK," he said as he lowered his rate. I continued for a few steps, until I realised my $ conversion was off, and he actually was charging $1. I felt so bad that I was trying to get the fortune-teller down to $1.

I first asked him if he spoke English. He said, "Yes," but that was far from the truth. I noticed some college kids nearby. I had generously donated to their fundraising the day before, so I figured, for another donation, they could translate.

The fortune-teller proceeded to look at my left hand, and through the nice college girl translating, I was told, "You are no good with husbands!" Good Lord! This was what the last two medicine men also told me! Yes, and he said I will have a third husband! I was definitely getting my $1's worth of advice. He also relayed that I would have a bad fall down a mountain, and he showed me on my wrist where the lines indicated this. He also recreated the mountain and my fall with animated hands.

I'm not sure if this dreadful advice meant I was going to have another horrible mountain fall, or if it was replaying the recent mountain crash. Either way, I decided to avoid the motorbike ride to the stupa the next day. It also made me rethink renting a motorbike in the near future.

After a few more innocuous observations from the fortune-teller, I decided I had definitely heard my money's worth! And I gave him a whopping 40-cent tip!

Nepal, 2018 – Trekking the Himalayas

When I arrived in Kathmandu, Nepal, I decided I wanted to go on an adventure trekking around the base of the world-famous Himalayan mountains.

The Himalayas are called the world's mightiest mountains that contain eight of the highest mountain peaks in the world. The name Himalaya derives from the Sanskrit name 'abode of snow'. The mountains stretch 1,553 miles (2,500km) across India, Nepal, Bhutan, China, and Pakistan. Travel legend has it, that it is only for the 'great adventurers and mountaineers', and is a place like no other. It is remote, majestic and romantic.

The area of the Himalayas is roughly ten times the area of France. Mt Everest gets most of the headlines as the tallest point on our planet at 29,000 feet (8,848 metres). In the mountain range, there are over 50 mountains higher that 23,000 ft (7,200 metres).

Everest was first climbed in 1953 when tourism and trekking tourism didn't exist. Today, about 35,000 tourists visit the region to trek or climb the Himalayan region. The area is inhabited by 53 million people from India, Nepal, Bhutan, China and Pakistan.

Although the views are spectacular, the region is also incredibly culturally diverse. The four distinct cultural groups are Hindu (Indian), Buddhist (Tibetan), Islamic (Afghanistan-Iran), and Animist (Burmese and South-eastern Asia). It is an area where the people are highly religious. Hinduism, Buddhism, and Islam are practiced. There is also a small number of Christians. It is said that they are among the most culturally diverse in the world.

The Annapurna region is the most diverse and popular region to trek in Nepal. There are treks of up to three weeks on the Annapurna circuit. Its highest mountains are at 27,000 feet (8,000 metres).

Guidebooks and experienced travellers will advise getting an experienced guide and using porters.

Hiring a porter does not mean you are weak and won't carry your belongings. It means you respect the Nepali culture and are providing the porter's family with an income. Guides and porters are invaluable in difficult conditions like fog, storms, zero visibility, and low temperatures. They will also acquire permits and travel documents.

It also is a great way of discovering and learning about the local customs, traditions and events are important in the locals' lives. I think I now know about everything there is to know about my guide's mountain village life, all his extended family and all their customs!

I had a great four-day trekking experience on the Annapurna circuit called the Ghorepani Poon Hill trek. It is voted by trekkers and guides as the best trekking route in the world. The peak of the trek is 10,531 feet (3,210 metres) and the sights, culture and experience are outstanding. Waking up in a basic, but clean, small inn, perched on the side of the mountain, and opening your window to the clear, magnificent view of the Himalayas is truly a moment to remember.

The mountains are full of life and many, many small villages. I saw mountain schools, farms, shops and lots of livestock. 58 miles (93km) later, I had seen some of the most breath-taking, interesting sights of my life. I truly recommend any adventurer to experience the Himalayas once in their lifetime!

Pokhara, 2018 – The Crash

After an exhilarating four-day trekking adventure through the Ghorepani Poon Hill area of the Himalayas, I decided to try my first experience at paragliding before heading to Kathmandu to volunteer at an orphanage.

My trekking guide recommended a delightful, 32-year-old, compactly built paragliding pilot named Yubraj. The next morning, he packed up his gear and we headed for the top of the local mountain in Sarankot to 5,300 feet (1,600 metres) in altitude. The sky was a bit hazy with intermittent winds. I watched 15 of the paragliding pilots take-off, running with their customers strapped to the front of the twosome. It looked so much fun and exhilarating.

Yubraj and I were up next. We had helmets on, and he carefully hooked all the safety gear in place. He then told me, "Run, when I say run." The large yellow and white parachute sail filled with wind. "Run!" he said. I ran four steps, and observed the sail falling to the ground in front of us. But our momentum was going forward, downhill! Tumble, crash, bush, another bush, roll, crash into bush. Upon finally stopping, which seemed to take a long time, I was horrified to look at my broken leg.

All the other paragliders, waiting to take off, were also was surprised and concerned too. I immediately shouted, "Get me to a hospital. FAST!" Thirty minutes later I was on a hospital bed with a shot of pain killer. Eight hours later I was operated on. The third world hospital conditions were rudimentary at best. Fortunately, the doctors and the anaesthesiologist spoke English and kept up my faith in the upcoming operation.

Days later, my son Benjie reassured me via text that these orthopaedic doctors were probably quite experienced and skilled in surgeries due to the high volume of mountain accidents from trekking and mountain climbing. He had a very good point!

I had never broken a bone in my life! This was all a new experience to me. I also feel quite fortunate that I only broke a leg. I feel that my athleticism and being in good physical shape helped prevent me from far worse damage. The result could have been much more devastating. I did thank God, and sent up many prayers for not making my situation worse! This was not what I had in mind for my last day before starting with the orphans in Kathmandu.

Well, sometimes life and God tells you to slow down! Surgery, three days of hospitalisation, and six weeks on crutches. My family and friends were horrified, and suggested I come back home to the USA to recover. I didn't give it much thought. I had come too far in my volunteer year, and was still committed to the orphanages in Nepal. As well-meaning as my family and friends were, I decided to stay in Nepal.

I found a quiet, local inn with a lovely garden and wonderfully staffed and started my six-week recovery. After having my backpack lost, and most of my clothes for the laundry stolen, days after my accident, I had to laugh. This was a cruel joke and my patience was being tested. The Nepalese Hindu gods surely did not like me!

When I stopped laughing, I realised I really didn't need that many clothes, and my recently found backpack would be many pounds lighter. I was truly thankful that my accident wasn't a lot worse. At least, I had the option to stay in Nepal and continue to help underprivileged kids.

The hospital systems are quite different in Nepal from the Western world, in that a family member must be responsible for the patient care from purchasing medicine, to providing food to emptying urine bags.

I must say that my pilot Yubraj, his family and the paragliding company did a remarkable job caring for me during my hospital stay and recovery for six weeks. I choose to look at that difficult time as a positive. I became very good friends with many locals. I enjoyed their stories and asked many questions about their lives. I learned so much about the Nepali culture and my new friends' daily challenges.

Hobbling on crutches for six weeks prohibited me from volunteering at an orphanage, as it was difficult to venture very far. Taxi rides were difficult over the pothole filled streets of Pokhara and were best saved for weekly doctor visits.

After many conversations with locals, I realised I could help the local underprivileged kids by helping them pay for school fees. Yubraj and I came up with a plan to help underprivileged kids in his remote village, as well as a family in great need from another part of the mountain.

Sri Lanka, 2012-2018 – The Head Wobble

After a few days in Nepal I was reminded of a custom I had last witnessed in great numbers in India and Sri Lanka. The mystery of the 'Head Wobble'. It is a cultural phenomenon that completely mystifies the Western world. Better known as the 'Wobble, Bobble or Head Shake', it is a source of much confusion and wonderment to foreigners.

It is even far more confusing when there are no words to go with the bobble. It is a cross between a shake and a nod. But does it mean Yes, No or Maybe? It is also contagious, and becomes quite infectious for people visiting Nepal, India and Sri Lanka. Many visitors have unconsciously caught themselves bobbling, including myself, in response to a bobbler.

Apparently, it is a non-verbal response to the Hindi word 'achha', and can mean anything from the word 'good' to 'Yes, I understand'. The most common usage is the affirmative, and an acknowledgment of 'I understand'. It can also be a substitute for 'Thank you'.

Not surprisingly there are also regional distinctions of head bobblers, and different speeds of head bobbling. Just to add utter confusion to the dilemma, it is also used in place of a 'no', when a person doesn't want to say 'no'.

There is a legend that claims the head bobble started in 1858 as the British ruled India, and the Indians were afraid to upset the British by saying 'no', so they chose to respond to them with the absolutely confusing… head bobble!

I have gone many wrong directions as I misinterpret the bobble, as in, "Is the train station that way?" I noticed my daughter Alex is very quick to pick up the bobble as we volunteer in bobbling countries. She is also very slow to lose her bobble upon returning home. It adds complete confusion to her responses to her friends when they ask if she wants to go to a party.

I am quite certain I have completely misinterpreted the bobble and have totally pissed off people that think I am doing the total opposite of their interpretation of the bobble. I get a huge laugh from standing out of hearing range and watching locals conduct wildly animated conversations while bobbling. I have absolutely no idea how they know what each other is saying.

This is just another of the completely charming things I love about Nepal, India and Sri Lanka!

Pokhara, 2018 – The Mountain Village Kids

My paragliding pilot and new friend Yubraj and I came up with a plan to help out some underprivileged kids. Helping to pay for school fees seemed like a very good use of money, while I was bedridden and recovering. I learned stories about the obstacles that many local kids had in just getting to and from school.

These kids live in mountainous areas and often have to walk one to two hours, each way, to attend school. Many times, they have to cross a river that may not have a bridge. I heard stories of how some kids hold their backpacks above their heads and walk-through rivers on their journey to school, getting soaked.

Often, the kids have to walk in the morning darkness to arrive on time. There is no money or resources for flashlights. There are no roads in most of the mountain villages. Walking is a part of their daily lives. It is nothing out of the ordinary, and a necessary part of going to school.

While there are some state schools, there is still money needed for uniforms, books, and possibly lunch. Where there is not a state school, there are fees needed to pay teachers and expenses. Most of the parents of these mountain kids are simple farmers, and well under the poverty level of income.

The reality of Nepal is that it is an extremely mountainous country with a small amount of flat, farmable land. The mountain people do their best to farm on terraced areas on the sides of the mountains. One farmer told me he can only farm enough to feed his family of four, and that there is minimal produce left to earn additional money. He felt privileged that he had a cow for milk and a dozen chickens to sell for some revenue.

I had the unique experience to go to the remote mountain area, on the back of a motorbike. It was excruciating hitting a pothole every few minutes, but well worth the pain. I stocked up on candy and soda to meet some of the kids. Usually I try not to give away sweets, as it contributes to tooth decay, but these kids rarely, if ever, have sweets, so I felt it was OK as a treat.

The first gaggle of kids I met were all happy, smiling, curious and outgoing kids. I'm not sure these kids had ever seen a big White lady like me. They were thrilled with the treats and we spoke some English and did some counting games. The mums crouched shyly off to the corner with the babies. But they too were curious, and eventually smiled and laughed with us. All these villagers lived in small, crude one room spaces with no running water.

Cooking was usually over a wood fire, and their diet consisted of rice and whatever vegetable was in season. There is no refrigeration, and any kind of meat is a rare delicacy. My observation of most of the kids in Nepal is that there are many small and thin kids due to meagre nutrition. Milk is a rare occurrence as it is rare to own a goat or cow.

The next family that I was sponsoring was an hour hike up the mountain from where I met them. I was so impressed that the mum walked her six-year-old girl, an hour down the mountain to meet me for a short visit, then headed back up the mountain to home. I was told that the 30-year-old dad chose not to go far with his education, when he was a young boy, and now he has a wife and two kids that he can barely feed by farming.

My next adventure on the motorbike was to go visit a family of eight, who are living a subsistent life. This required a 45-minute motorbike ride and a 20-minute climb down the side of the mountain to their crude home. They felt lucky to be there, as the generous land owner allowed the family to reside there and farm part of the land. He was even nice enough to purchase some goats for them to help them out. He is such a great example to follow.

They were the poorest of the poor. They also had a 'special needs' child among the six kids ranging in age from 4-16. I'm not sure the parents had much, if any schooling. Talking through a translator, they could not even remember how old each kid was. The eight-year-old girl was so excited I was visiting and proudly showed me how she cares for the four goats. After a few minutes, the mum, dad, and four of the kids came from the fields. The kids that were farming with the parents looked to be about 10 years old up to the 16-year-old eldest boy.

I have observed in many of these cultures, the underprivileged kids do not have toys to play with. It was also noticeable in the local shops that there were little to no shops selling balls and toys. It is just not part of the culture, and there certainly isn't the money to buy such items. When I would see a few kids playing games, it was usually with rocks, sticks, leaves and other things found in nature. Most of these families do not have running water or electricity. A TV is an extreme rarity.

At any river side, there are several women doing laundry as well as washing their kids. They have a different view of hygiene than Westerners do, as water is a scarce commodity and difficult to transport by foot.

The body odour of the teens and adults is of no concern for these people, and dental care is hit or miss. They would probably be alarmed at the Western standards and obsession with cleanliness, as we are with theirs.

The mountain kids are among the most resilient kids I've ever witnessed. There is little to no crying, the kids entertain themselves, are respectful to their families and appear to live in the moment.

The family entity is the key to the survival in this culture. Rarely does a family member venture outside the family for life experiences. The exception is the young men over 18 years of age, who often travel to other countries to work in low-paying jobs. They usually sign two-year contracts, working in construction, manual labour, the service industry or other low skilled jobs, in order to send money home to their families.

Upon flying to Kathmandu and landing at the airport, I witnessed my plane was 60% filled with young men under 30, fashionably dressed, arriving back home from their jobs abroad. It also explained the large numbers of men picking up medium-sized well wrapped TVs, from the baggage claim. Clearly, this was a treat for their families to own a TV.

Pokhara, 2018 – The Future of the Young People

As one of the 10% poorest countries in the world, the Nepalese young people have a difficult time dreaming about education and success in their future. Of the young ladies, there is incessant talk and discussions of weddings. Wedding attire, food for the wedding, guest list, jewellery, music, flowers, and time of year for the wedding. I did not understand this phenomenon, even after volunteering in India.

I now understand. My opinion is that it is extremely rare for a Nepalese young woman to go to university and further her education. I met several times with a bright, pretty 19-year-old Nepalese young woman from a poor family. Her English was very good. She approached me and wanted to know how she could get a job abroad and make money for her family. This goes against her culture, but her need to help the family financially, superseded the norm.

After coming up with several options in the next few days, she seemed quite happy to pursue the ideas I had for her. I asked her if she could drive, and she looked at me in horror! "No!" she said. I wished her the best and told her to contact me on social media with questions. She is the exception.

Most Nepalese young women will marry young. My local friends explained to me that most of the marriages in their area are arranged. They said about 75% of marriages, in their experience, are arranged. I spent hours listening to the stories of the young couples meeting for the first time, then marrying two weeks later. I was mortified but tried to not let it show.

One male, local friend, told me of his six meetings with young ladies that his family had chosen for him to marry. He turned down the first five. But number six was the charm. He now has school-age kids. I asked what made him decide on his sixth potential bride, who is now his wife? He told me, "She looked like she would be a good worker." What a romantic guy!

The young men in Nepal have a big challenge with the lack of jobs available close to their home or village. 69% of the labour force works in agriculture. Tourism, along with trekking and mountain climbing, is popular for jobs.

Speaking English is a requirement to get one of these coveted jobs.

I also discovered that tourism is seasonal and there is much downtime throughout the year in many of these jobs. As I witnessed at the airport on arrival and departing Nepal, there are many young men leaving the country to work in low-skilled, often low-paying jobs. It is reported that there is 40% unemployment among Nepalese men. Nearly four million Nepalese men, one quarter of the workforce, work abroad. One third of the country's GDP comes from overseas workers. The most popular work locations are Qatar, Malaysia, Singapore and other parts of the Middle East.

A young man may average roughly $200 a month, and most send as much as possible, after their living expenses, to their families in Nepal. Many of the business men I spoke to, did not marry until they were over 30 years old. They are also trending toward one or two children families. They said that it is just too expensive to raise a child, and they are choosing to keep their families small.

Crazy Travel Stories

India, New Delhi, 2012 – Okhla Phase II – Slums

It was July in New Delhi, India. The temperatures were a sweltering 113 degree (44 degrees C). My 16-year-old daughter Alex, myself, and three energetic, 24-year-old Scottish schoolteachers were volunteering in the slums of New Delhi. The school structure that we were volunteering at, consisted of a dusty, concrete slab with a corrugated tin-roof covering the pad. The toilet area was covered in dust, and filled with garbage and looked as if it had been years since it was functional.

Former volunteers had brightly painted the three walls, and managed to paint on a makeshift chalkboard. The roughly 150 students from the local slum neighbourhood traipsed in and out of the makeshift classroom at all times of the day. There was no class list, supplies, music, play area, grass, lighting or water. Yet, there were happy, energetic, enthusiastic, smiling, laughing kids! It was our job to teach English, the best we could.

On a good day there was a middle-aged male teacher sitting on a half-broken chair doing his best to teach the older kids science and math. Our job was to teach English to the Hindi speaking kids and do our best to engage them in learning. Very few kids knew how to speak English.

There was a very elderly woman. I would guess she was pushing 90 years. She came to the school most days wrapped in her vivid pink sari. She too, sat in a broken chair and observed the kids. She spoke no English, and our Hindi was limited, so we just figured she was probably the grandmother to a huge amount of the kids. She usually had a smile on her face. I think this is just how she passed her days!

We knew school and medical supplies were difficult to obtain locally, so we brought several duffle bags stuffed with supplies from home, in the USA. I always bring art supplies, clothing, hygiene items, games, puzzles, school books, colouring books, markers, glitter and balloons. It is fantastic for the kids, but is also self-serving in that it gives us projects and activities to do with the kids.

As volunteers, Scottish Jenny and USA Alex rolled on their plastic gloves and grabbed the antiseptic, Band-Aids, and calamine lotion, the line of kids with injuries started to form. Invariably, the gash or wound they wanted covered with the Band-Aid was easily visible, and far less severe than the wound they couldn't see, which needed much more attention.

The kids were fascinated with Band-Aids! At school, we established a daily hygiene time. Anyone could line up for attention to cuts, scrapes and wounds. Our goal was primarily to try to keep the wound clean and avoid infection.

The kids and their parents started referring to the girls as 'Dr Jenny' and 'Dr Alex'. We had many laughs, but continued to correct them, as the girls were just performing simple hygiene on the kids, and were indeed, not doctors.

Lice were a constant concern, and continuing problem. Most kids have many siblings and sleep in a communal bed. They tend to transfer lice back and forth to each other. We had lice shampoo days and helped with the combing of the lice nits and eggs. This was just part of the normal week. A weekly lice-killing shampoo was also part of our own personal hygiene. We also taught preventative measures for lice infestation.

One day a clean, well-dressed mum brought her 'special needs' young boy to the school. I knew that we had some 'special needs' kids and possibly this was a new student. Jenny was knee-deep in cleaning and caring for the line of kids and dealing with their wounds, cuts and replacing bandages. She saw the mother and her boy, took a deep breath and said to me in her adorable Scottish accent, "I'm pretty sure we don't have enough calamine lotion to fix that one!" Fortunately, the mum only spoke Hindi!

India, New Delhi, 2012 – Okhla Phase II – Sachine and the Tooth

Each day, the five of us volunteers took the 25-minute tuk tuk ride to the slums of New Delhi. We taught the kids in the makeshift, tin roof, open air, concrete platform that served as the classroom of the local school. Little six-year-old Sachine was a bright, active, scrappy kid. He was one of our favourite kids! He was always the first to arrive and the last to leave. It was pretty apparent that he loved all the volunteer teachers and the fun and excitement we brought. He was the first to help clean up, wear the silly cowboy hat, and try to solve the math problem or just sit quietly next to a volunteer hoping for a hug.

Sachine had a big wiggler of a loose front tooth that was about to fall out. Sixteen-year-old volunteer Alex helped wiggle it a bit, and by the next day at school, it popped out! He was so excited. He quickly jumped up and ran down the dusty, dirt filled small opening between the slum buildings to the outside ripped up street. He held on tight to his recently liberated front tooth. He then hurled it into the 6' (two metres) plumbing ditch that was knee deep with mosquitoes, mud, rocks and dirt. Satisfied, he ran back to join in with the group of six kids that Alex was reading to.

Alex had a precious, teachable moment, with a group of six to eight-year-old kids. She had brought a brightly coloured, sparkly book from home about the 'tooth fairy'. The six kids were enraptured listening to a fantastic tale about a fairy that comes to your house at night. Young Devi looked quite puzzled as they read from the book. She raised her little hand and asked Alex, "Is the tooth fairy a bird princess?"

"Well," said Alex, "Let's go with bird princess!"

Alex continued, "If your tooth comes out, you put it under your pillow at night and the 'bird princess' brings you money!" Sachine had a look of horror on his face. He jumped up and ran down the dirty alley, past the small opening, out to the mosquito filled ditch in search of his tooth. Unbelievably, 30 minutes later, Sachine proudly marched up to Alex with his tooth in hand.

An amazed Alex looked at me and we quickly scrambled to find 'bird princess' money in our backpacks. We produced 40 cents or $20. Realising 40 cents would probably do the job, Alex handed it over to Sachine. The proud look on his face was as if he had just won the lottery! The next early morning before school started, there was a line of little ones all wiggling their teeth hoping the 'bird princess' would come visit them!

India, New Delhi, 2012 – Oklah Phase II – Slums – Mani-Pedi

Volunteering in the slums of New Delhi was much more than just teaching English to the 150 kids that randomly passed through our modest school. We know the importance of teaching health and hygiene lessons, and do our best to get kids started on healthy habits at home. One of our hygiene lessons was teaching the importance of handwashing with soap and cleanliness of nails, as well as feet. The reality of the slums is that water is extremely scarce in this part of New Delhi and there are little to no toilet facilities.

We noticed that there was no running water in the slum. Every two days we would see the process of the village women lining up to capture water in their large plastic containers, from a temporary, pumped underground water source. We quickly understood how precious water was, and it explained a lot as to why the kids were for the most part, were pretty dirty and dusty.

There was no toilet available near the school. As for the teachers, the closest toilet was down the block at the fly infested lunch restaurant. It was typical for the kids to have

146

lice in their hair and dirty clothing, and bodies. This however, had no bearing on how happy, gregarious and fantastic the kids were. It is just the norm.

One of my favourite activities to do with the girls is 'Manicure Day'. That is also, using the term 'manicure' loosely. My teaching aim is to have them take pride in clean, polished nails. In our bags of supplies from home, I brought a colourful assortment of nail polish colours, new nail files, cotton balls, polish remover and orange sticks to help with the lesson. We also give away all the items after we finish, which is always appreciated by the girls.

The excitement grew as the first few girls proudly showed off their pink and blue beautifully painted nails. After about 10 of the girls were finished, a gaggle of four to five-year-old boys and girls wanted us to paint their nails. My teaching project was a hit!

Minutes later, a mum showed up, and in her best 'head bobble' wanted us to paint her nails. Sure! We're here for the community! Very quickly, word spread that it was manicure day in the village. The village mums quickly came out of hiding, and formed a line for their manicures. We had four volunteers, all painting nails that had definitely not seen soap or water in a long time. Mum #1 proceeded to head bobble me again and point at her feet.

I immediately pointed to Alex and said, "Alex is really good at pedicures. She'll do it for you." Alex became the most popular girl in the village that day! Oh, and right on track, they all came back the next week, for a touch up!

India, New Delhi, 2012 – Tuk Tuks

The most popular and very effective mode of transportation in New Delhi is the tuk tuk. In some areas they are known as auto rickshaws. Tuk tuks are small, fuel efficient, loud, open air, almost 'tin-can' like, motorbike-based vehicles. The name is derived from the sound the vehicles make as they sputter forward. They are made to hold three people, but it is not unusual to find families of eight stuffed in many tuk tuks!

Most are painted a bright lemon yellow and lime green colour. Hailing one is easy, but as a Westerner, negotiating the price of the ride is an exhausting and frustrating experience. By nature of being a non-local, the price goes up dramatically. Layer in the part about asking the driver to bring you to the most disturbing and devastatingly poor slums of New Delhi, the price to get to our volunteer school was three times what the rate should have been, no matter how much negotiating I tried. Many drivers laughed at me when I said, "Oklah Phase II," and quickly sped off. There was no way they we're going to put their lives in jeopardy. It was a daily hassle. In fairness to the tuk tuk drivers, getting a ride out of the slums seemed to be relatively easy and surprisingly, the normal price.

In many instances, the tuk tuks are a reflection of the drivers' personality and filled with decorations, religious icons, children's photos, and plastic floral concoctions. Some look like the inside of a Michael's craft store! The most fun rides are when the drivers turn up their upbeat, loud, Bollywood music!

Each of the tuk tuk experiences seems to be an entertainment in itself, before even looking out the open-air windows. Every caricature of a tuk tuk driver you have ever seen is not far from the truth!

An early morning 25-minute tuk tuk drive to the slums, from an upper middle-class part of town, is a gut-wrenching, disturbing, sad, depressing experience. It runs the range of dead bodies on the side of the road to 10-year-old girls selling their bodies, with mum encouraging them from behind. There are begging elderly and kids that surround the tuk tuk at almost each stop. It is highly advisable not to hand out money; it only perpetuates and encourages the begging.

I have had many helpless feelings in that I can't help each person that desperately needs money for food, shelter and clothing. The best us volunteers can do is teach and help the kids and the community for the time period we are there. We hopefully brighten their day and spark their love of learning, and create new learning experiences. For the most fun tuk tuk ride, keep an open mind, smile at the driver and hang on for dear life! Oh, and rock out to the Bollywood music!

India, New Delhi Slums, 2012 – Okhla Phase II – Home Visits

I truly believe that most kids love, respect and admire their teachers. We six volunteers, three of us from the USA and three from Scotland, were definitely feeling the love from these energetic, sweet, appreciative kids. By week two, some of the kids were asking us to come after school to visit their homes and meet their mums.

Not exactly sure, how to approach this, we decided we should give it a try. We didn't want to have the kids think badly of us, so we said we could do a quick visit to one of the 'special needs' boy's home. Off we went the next day in the oppressive heat. I was also so curious to see the insides of the homes that our kids lived in.

Walking up the larger street, we noticed a butcher on the side of the road with his push cart. Oh my God!!! There were 10,000 flies buzzing on top of the uncovered meat he was trying to sell. We had never seen anything like it. No wonder the six of us were continually sick with diarrhoea, if that was the hygiene standard.

After passing winding alleys filled with stench, faeces, kids running around without clothes on, and some people trying to pump water, we reached little Dev's house. His mum met us at the doorway and was so proud to show off the room that they ate and lived in. She was gracious and offered us hot tea, which we took and drank. There was definitely a language barrier, but Dev could translate some.

She then showed us the sleeping room next door. The family of six seemed to sleep on a platform with a quilt, and a piece of cardboard placed on the floor. It now made sense why lice infestation was so rampant. They slept multi-generational in extremely tight quarters.

We smiled and thanked the family for their hospitality and told them how much we enjoyed Dev in class and that that he was a great kid.

A few days later Alex and I went to another student's house. Puja was so proud to have her teachers at her home for a visit. Her home was a one room, dangerously hot home with no circulation or windows, just a door. She was from a family of eight and there, also, were only two sleeping surfaces. Some of the family slept on the ground. Puja's mum had invited us for tea. I noticed the modest tea kettle was placed on top of two bricks, and there was a small piece of coal igniting a fire to heat the kettle.

Little Puja was happy we were visiting and her mum gave her some sort of biscuits to pass to us. My stomach could just see the word 'vomit' on the biscuit, and I carefully hid the biscuit behind me on a shelf.

"Oh, there's your biscuit!" said Puja. I was so busted, and had to eat it. And yes, I got sick from the food. But we were really glad to see how the kids lived. These visits made them so proud, that a teacher thought highly enough of them, that we would come meet their families.

World travellers will debate many topics, but I have always heard everyone agree that India has the craziest travel stories ever! Nothing even compares!

India, New Delhi Slums, 2010 – Zoo Trip

One of my joys of helping kids is taking them on an adventure. In the slums of Delhi in Okhla-Phase II, at our small, shack of a makeshift school, with its corrugated tin roof, and concrete slab foundation, 150 kids passed through our school each day. This served as the local, government supported school for the surrounding government-built slums.

There was no running water at the school, or surrounding area. It was also a record setting heatwave that June and the temperatures were a scalding 113 degrees (44 degrees C).

Where there had once been a toilet, it was now a dry, dirty, dusty hole in the ground with garbage piled on top.

There were no supplies, desks, books or teaching aids of any kind. There was a state-paid male teacher, and a male head of the program. Fortunately, we had brought many bags of supplies, books, games, artwork, paper, workbooks and some fun toys.

The kids had so much fun drawing, spelling, doing math, creating artwork, reading and playing games. We were a big hit with the kids and they waited anxiously as our tuk tuk pulled up each morning. They jumped up and down and squealed in delight as we walked through the narrow pathway to the concrete slab of a school.

We ran strings zig-zagging near the ceiling and taped up their artwork, drawings, spelling tests and math worksheets. The kids were so proud of their work and pointed it out to all their friends. We brought many toothbrushes and tubes of toothpaste and did 'teeth cleaning' and 'hygiene days'. The early teen girls also were given a talk about menstruating by a volunteer, an older woman who spoke Hindi.

We did 'lice days' and helped wash and comb out the kids' hair with lice shampoo. We volunteers also did a weekly lice shampoo treatment on our hair, as we had kids climbing all over us all day, and there was a high likelihood we were getting infected with lice.

The kids were from the poorest families I had ever seen in my life. This however, did not dampen their joy and enthusiasm for learning and speaking English! I would probably say these kids were the most appreciative of any kids we have ever worked with.

We announced to the kids, that in a week, we were all going to take a bus and go to the local zoo and science museum. The majority of these kids had never been out of their neighbourhood, and were filled with excitement. They made drawings of animals, and made a poster announcing their school name and 'Zoo trip!'

On zoo trip day, the old, rickety bus was packed with every neighbourhood schoolkid who had ever attended the school. There were kids piled on each other's laps and hanging out the windows. This day was an adventure of a lifetime for the kids. Each of us six volunteers tried to gather up a group to look after, but it was pretty crazy. These kids ran from animal to animal, and had the best time ever! We did a lunch on the grass and played lots of games, then as a surprise, went to the science museum. It was packed with cool experiments, funny exhibits, silly distorting mirrors and it was air conditioned. We were all in heaven!

Upon returning at the late end of the day, the kids said that was the most fun they've ever had! Back to more lice treatments tomorrow!

India, New Delhi, 2012 – The Subway

The hot weekends in New Delhi were tortuous in the 113 degrees (44 degrees C) heat. The Lonely Planet guide book suggested the best way to cool off in the dreadful summers in New Delhi was to ride the subway. Can you imagine telling a New Yorker that? So we picked a tourist attraction and headed for the subway. There were eight of us international volunteers, from everywhere: from Kazakhstan, to Germany, the USA and Scotland. Most of the girls were mid-twenties and volunteering, as they were on holiday or between teaching jobs.

As we entered the air-conditioned subway cars, we were ecstatic to finally be cooling down. Some of us had a fan in our windowless, un-air-conditioned sleeping room, but with the power cuts and the heat, the fans weren't effective.

The stares we were getting on the subway, from the male riders, were absurd. We noticed a huge percentage of men and boys on the subway. Well, we figured the women in their society were generally at home taking care of the kids. We definitely didn't say anything and tried to ignore all the attention. Yes, the volunteer girls were exotic and lovely, but had these guys never seen a pretty girl!

This subway behaviour went on for a month. We didn't take the subway daily, but would take it on weekends. It wasn't until our last day of our 30 days volunteering that we entered the subway and saw a bright pink car in the front of the train marked in both Hindi and English 'Women's Car!'

I felt like a complete idiot! And I take back all the mean thoughts I had about the men staring at us!

Sri Lanka, Galle, 2015 – The 'Special Needs' Girls and Tea

In Sri Lanka, we were lucky to get to help teach a group of about 20 'special needs' girls for many mornings. It had been many years since I had volunteered with 'special needs' girls, and it was 19-year-old Alex and Nicole's first experience. Many of the teaching techniques were the same as other kids, there were just more unpredictable, emotional and challenging issues from these kids. We did lots of colouring, games, sports, dances and artwork.

The kids loved music and dancing. Nicole even brought many T-shirts from her kind bosses from the organic restaurant and juice bar where she worked at back home, in Tucson, Arizona. The girls were delighted with their new T-shirts, and happily danced and posed for photos.

One of the most challenging girls had a rare, unconditional reflex where she spit at people. Our sweet 50-year-old teacher explained the condition to us, and we said it wouldn't bother us. Easier said than done! We now laugh at how many times we were spat on and tried to pretend that nothing was wrong.

Alex would even give us her daily tally of how many times she deflected the spit. It didn't seem to dampen the day; it's just that we ran for the shower at the end of those days.

Our sweet, amazingly calm teacher, Mrs Sada, immediately liked us and enjoyed the diversity we brought to the classroom. We too, had fun with the kids. After a couple of weeks, she invited us to her house for tea. It was a very kind gesture, and as much as we exhausted at the end of a volunteer day, but we wanted to be polite. I'm not sure how Nicole squirmed out of it, but Alex and I agreed to go. Mrs Sada's 18-year-old son was thrilled to be driving Alex on his motorbike through the streets of Galle, with her long blond hair flowing, to the teacher's house. At the teacher's house, we met her husband and they both spoke English very well.

We politely drank our tea and ate our biscuits and asked many questions about how the couple met and their lives. They produced a wedding album and we tediously went through each page with them. They told us much detail about the wedding of many years ago. Then, Mrs Sada went to her computer and skyped her 26-year-old son, who was working as an engineer in Qatar.

Oh My God! This was a total set up! Alex was mortified, but polite, as the computer was handed to her to talk to her future husband. She looked sideways at me and asked me, "What do I say?"

I was chuckling to myself and said, "Just ask him about himself and his work."

The 10-minute, excruciating conversation, ended when there was a power cut, and we told our hosts we had a lovely time, but we needed to get back. "Oh, but we can continue the conversation on the phone," she said. Even the motorbike driving son seemed to be mortified about his mum's actions.

I awkwardly explained to our hosts that in our country, young girls often go on to college to further their education and most do not get married until after 30. She seemed so deflated, but resigned to the fact that Alex would not be their future daughter-in-law. Alex and motorbike son had a big laugh at the evening as he dropped her back home!

Sri Lanka, Galle, 2015 – The Muslim Girls

Another of our many interesting volunteer placements was the 'after school program' for the Muslim girls. Alex and Nicole headed the program three afternoons a week and I joined them as I could. The program was primarily to learn English, but could be whatever Alex and Nicole wanted to do with the time.

Interestingly enough, the program was for any of the Muslim schoolkids, but other than a few 12-year-old boys, was made up of about 16 girls. After some whiteboard

English lessons, it was time for games, music and artwork. Alex, Nicole and I brought lots of artwork supplies one day and proceeded to hand out the colourful paper, glitter, sparkly glue, ribbons, brightly coloured pipe cleaners and other fun supplies.

The girl's faces looked delighted. "OK," we said "Make whatever you want to out of your treasures." There was silence. Nobody was diving into their art project. What did we do wrong? Alex then picked up some paper and started to draw a design on the paper. The girls all looked inquisitive. At that moment we realised these girls had not done artwork with these kinds of supplies, and they didn't know where to start.

With a little encouragement, they dove in. About an hour later, I had never seen such a beautiful display of lovely design, sparkle and creativity. They were so proud of their creations and we encouraged them to take them home and show their families.

We were later told that the girls loved to come to 'after school English class' because it let them be kids, and have a break from the routine housework and child care, as was customary at home.

The Muslim girls blossomed in a month and by our last day, the grassy field was filled with the girls playing sports. This love of sports had been foreign to them a month earlier. They happily sang and chased each other around the field. There were often, many of the older school boys sitting off to the side of the field looking quite envious!

Sri Lanka, Galle, 2015 – The Nursery and the Bakery Girls

Seventeen-year-old Alex and Nicole and I were headed to Galle, in the south of Sri Lanka to volunteer. I never know what experiences lay ahead, and I have learned to keep a very open mind. I also like to help out in the areas of greatest need. I feel a greater sense of accomplishment by doing that.

This volunteer adventure was unique from prior countries and volunteer placements, in that we were going to be rotating and helping several different ages and groups in need. We were excited, as the various placements would keep us extremely busy and the month would fly by.

We started in a children's orphanage which housed about 26 orphans that seemed to be under three years old. As I crossed through the grassy area to get to the building that the kids slept in, I stepped, a few different times, on what I thought was dog poop. But I didn't see any dogs. I figured they were busy with the kids and didn't have time to pick up the dog poop.

The four volunteer girls and I were horrified as we entered the orphanage. There were 20 iron cribs lined up with slats of wood on the bottom. There were no mattresses, toys, pillows, bedding or anything but the bare horrible cribs.

As we looked around at 26 kids, they were corralled in a 15' x 15' (4.6m x 4.6m) corner, most without diapers or bottoms of any kind on. These kids were half dressed. There was also what appeared to be an older physically handicapped girl of about six, tied into her crib by a cloth. Most of the kids had very short hair or shaved heads. I believed it could have been a lice outbreak, but couldn't be sure.

There was an unusual amount of tears from the kids and they were running chaotically around the baby pen area. We were instructed not to pick up the kids, but we could play with them in the pen. I asked why we couldn't pick kids up and was told, rudely and abruptly, "That's the way it is, and do NOT take any photos of anything!"

The five of us sat in the child playpen and gently played with the kids, as they were a bit shy. Then one of the girls mentioned that she just got peed on. As that was happening, other kids were peeing on the floor. Soon the kids were slipping on the pee and hurting themselves. That started another round of multiple crying and wailing.

We later asked if we could take the kids outside for fresh air and to play on the grass. Begrudgingly, the few caregivers let us. I soon realised that the poop I had stepped on was that of the kids. We asked if we could take the crib-bound six-year-old girl out for some sunshine and were told, "NO, she stays in her crib all the time." This place was a house of horrors and nobody seemed to care.

I saw two of the volunteers, later, ask a caregiver a question, and I heard the caregiver shouting at the volunteers. This was unacceptable. The girls were in tears. We all hated every aspect of the orphanage.

Upon our return to our lodging, we wanted to speak to the owner of the company we had volunteered through. We told him of the horrible situation at the orphanage and the fact that there were no diapers on the kids. He calmly explained that he was powerless to do anything about it. He said that it was well-known that the head woman at the orphanage takes the money for diapers, and sells donated diapers and she keeps the money. We were all horrified, but decided to stay for the balance of the week and see if we could help out with the kids.

The rest of the days were equally bad as each volunteer was scolded for picking up kids, comforting kids and giving the kids love and attention. I saw each volunteer cry, including myself, as we were yelled at. This was insanely unfair.

After five days of hopelessness, and watching each volunteer cry in frustration, we told the volunteer company we all refuse to be in such an abusive situation and will not be going back to the orphanage. The very sad thing was that the kids would suffer as a result, but we could not continue in that 'House of Horror'. We all want to believe that karma will take care of the horrible woman!

We spent several days a week working with teenage girls at what was called a 'Girls' Home'. There seemed to be 40 girls ranging from 12-17. We found out that many of these girls were placed here as detention from their families that believed the girls to be 'bad girls'.

I found out that four of the girls were considered to be bad because they had become pregnant and gave birth to their babies. Those babies were currently in the 'House of Horrors' nursery. More disturbing, the extremely young girls that had given birth, had been raped by family members, but were considered outcasts and placed in the girls' home.

These girls were not like any young teens I had ever experienced. There seemed to be several girls with mental health problems, many with tough, argumentative personalities, and most of the girls had deep survival instincts.

Smart, pretty, kind, volunteer, Nynke, from the Netherlands, had been working with the girls for two months on a 'Self-Esteem and Girl Empowerment' project, for her college internship at her university back home. She gave us many insights into the daily routines and educational projects she was working on with the girls.

One of the best success stories was the Bakery Girls. It was a group of 12 of the best behaved, smartest, and hardest working of the 40 girls. The Bakery Girls' Project was started by a local baker, who donated her time and money to teach the girls a marketable skill. Then, as they reached the age of 18, when they could no longer stay in the home, they would have a marketable skill. The goal was that upon leaving the Girls' Home, they would become employed and independent; hopefully avoid a life of poverty.

Three afternoons a week, the girls spent hours creating wonderful treats, learning teamwork, and having pride in their accomplishments. Us volunteers were the recipients of all the tasty treats and wonderful breads. After their baking, four of the volunteer young girls helped them with their English and played games and taught 'self-help' tools and information. The common denominator I saw with all the girls from the girls' home, was the low self-esteem they each seemed to have. The Bakery Girls seemed to be the most confident and outspoken of the group and did derive a sense of pride from their work.

For the Bakery Girls, it also allowed them to get out of the Girls' Home several times a week, and stimulate them. Alex and Nicole, who were very good Club Volleyball players at their schools and clubs in the USA, decided to teach rules, regulations, technique and sportsmanship to the girls. It was a good call, and the girls were fiercely competitive. It was a great place to channel the girls' energy and emotions. But the weak did not survive out on the volleyball court! It was a game for only the toughest of the girls.

Three mornings a week, we went to a Christian Elderly Folks home to entertain, care for, and just chat with the elderly women who did not have families that could care for them. There were several former nuns, and a handful spoke passable English. Alex, Nicole and I had not worked with the elderly before, but how hard could it be? In a way, it was like dealing with pre-schoolers. It was really great, as I was certainly not that many decades from their age. Some of the women were completely incapacitated.

We quickly realised many liked music, artwork, puzzles, cards, craft projects, chatting, and getting lotion rubbed on their hands and feet. We just made-up activities as we went along. We were greeted with huge smiles and happy faces each day as we arrived. Some told stories of their lives and childhoods, others drooled and smiled. They grew to love our visits and it was a fantastic experience.

Two afternoons a week, Australian, Becca and I went to the local Nursing College and did two-hour English conversation classes. In front of us were 75 of the smartest, young students on the Island of Sri Lanka. They were extremely respectful and hung on to our every word. The professor would start a lesson, then after a few minutes, turn it over to us, as he was in unfamiliar territory. I decided to make this into a fun, noisy, active, competitive English conversation lesson. Not some dull, sentence diagramming class.

The nursing students' class was at the dreadful 2–4 pm slot in the day. I witnessed several heads nodding off that first day while the professor was doing his best at the white board. My solution was to send the students for a wake-up run.

They had never experienced anything like it! I told them to stand up, walk out the door and follow me on a run. It was hilarious watching the girls hold onto their nursing hats as they ambled down the street, rounded the corner and headed back. Nobody nodded off after that. They actually started to like the wake-up runs!

Our biggest success was splitting the students off into groups of eight, and speaking to each other in English about subjects they were interested in. They already had a handle on the technical terms they needed, but started making real progress on conversation English.

I asked about their families, hopes for the future and about boyfriends or girlfriends. That really had everyone talking. We also incorporated fun board games of word recognition and had them competing for the best team. These bright young men and women were great! If I'm ever in a hospital in Sri Lanka, hopefully one of my students is taking care of me!

Sri Lanka, Weligama, 2015 – Free Willy

I usually don't get excited about whale watching. I have always found it an overrated tourist thing to do. I have often laughed at the old folks that day after day sit and claim to see whales migrate. To me, it's the ocean equivalent of bird watching, or worse, watching paint dry. But we were told that in this particular part of southern Sri Lanka, lived an exotic type of whale that was indigenous to this location.

With an open mind and sense of adventure, Alex, Nicole and I ventured out for our five-hour whale watching trip. It was a sunny morning with huge waves rocking the boat. I knew that the calmest part of the boat was where the boat Captain was, steering the boat. That was on the top, centre of the medium-sized boat of about 60 tourists. We were told we had to venture at least one and a half hours south in the Indian Ocean to see the spectacular whales.

As I looked to my left as we were leaving the harbour, I saw the strangest fishing boat with enormous masts bobbing up and down the same direction we were going. Upon closer inspection I could see the 10–12 raggedy fishermen.

Four were atop the masts, shouting to the others below. As we got closer, I could almost swear this looked like a pirate ship with Keith Richards and Johnny Depp out to plunder an innocent ship. It was a bit creepy, but I learned this was a normal sighting.

After about 30 minutes, I noticed many of the tourists turning pale, and running for the lower back of the boat. This was not good! More and more left the rocking and bobbing top level of the boat. An excited crewman shouted to the passengers, that up ahead, was a whale!

The few remaining passengers seemed relieved to finally see a whale. "Oh, you mean a whale back one foot above the water," I said. Chasing the whales went on for an hour, and I saw several whale backs. This seemed to suffice for the boat Capitan, and we turned around to head back. It was a long rocky, boat ride back to shore.

We hadn't seen Nicole for a long time. Apparently, she was downstairs at the back of the boat getting sick with the throngs of others. It seemed to be contagious. After finishing the day, Nicole told us she didn't get to see any whales. Poor thing. All that misery for nothing! And when I told her, Alex and I saw some backs of whales she said, "What did you think you were going to see? Free Willy jumping through hoops at Sea World?" She had a very good point!

Morocco, Rabat, 2016 – Ramadan

When asked where she wanted to volunteer in the coming summer, 20-year-old Alex said, "Morocco!" The land of exoticism, deserts, mosques and camels.

"Sure," I said. A few days later I told her "The good news is we're going to volunteer in Morocco, the bad news is it's Ramadan."

Strangely, unfamiliar to us, we quickly googled it. We decided to make the best of it and enjoy the local customs and all the peculiarities, to us, that came with it. We were no stranger to heat, humidity, mosquitoes, bad food, diarrhoea, funky illnesses and lots of kids' snot on us!

"Let's give it a go!" we decided. We did our best to become honorary Muslims. We respected the Muslim rules and traditions of Ramadan month. Primarily, not eating until sundown.

Our lovely Muslim host family provided us with a plentiful 'Iftar' meal, as we arrived on day one of Ramadan. When asked if we wanted to be served the midnight meal and the three-thirty a.m. meal, we politely declined. We were volunteering with 22 rambunctious little kids during the day, and needed every minute of sleep we could get.

We quickly realised that we were starving by five p.m. each day. I don't know how the locals do this. But they were eating two additional meals throughout the night that we were not. It seemed as if the day was just flipped upside down. But someone had to care for the kids, and that was our job.

We were in a medium size town north of Casablanca, called Rabat. Rabat is the capital of Morocco, with the urban population of over 1.2 million people. It was listed by CNN in 2013 as second best of 'Top Travel Destinations of 2013'. It is also listed as a World Heritage Site. It was commutable to Casablanca and the trains were filled each day with the working people.

We were an extreme oddity, as Westerners being in Morocco during Ramadan. 99% of Moroccans are Muslim. Other than our volunteer group of 10, I did not see more than five non-locals in the month we were there.

Our weekdays were filled with caring for, entertaining, playing with, feeding, comforting, and playing mum to the 22 kids. Armed with balloons, bubbles, jump ropes and balls, we had a blast with the kids. We grew to really love these kids, even the tough ones.

Lunch time was painful, because we were starving and had to look at the food the kids were eating. The custom is that during Ramadan, one may not drink water between sunrise and sunset. We were so hot with the temperature in the high 80 F (27 degrees C), and decided this was not our religion, and we were going to secretly drink water. But we had to be careful that nobody saw us.

After school, we then found a tea house where we could sit and rest. They were not supposed to serve us before sundown, due to Muslim rules. But they were very compassionate, and they felt sorry for us, and served us tea each afternoon while we waited for sundown.

We also had a few Iftar meals on the beaches of Rabat, and it was a glorious scene watching all the miserable, hungry people turn back into pleasant human beings after eating and drinking. Alcohol was strictly forbidden. That sucked, too!

Exploring Morocco on the weekend trips was great fun. There is an efficient train system that runs fairly reliably. It was a great way to see beautiful Morocco!

Morocco, Zagora Desert, 2016 – Camels

After a five-hour train ride through Morocco, the eight of us volunteers were in the Southern Moroccan Desert, in Zagora. It is a beautiful landscape unlike anything most people have seen in real life. It is almost Hollywood cliché in its depiction of endless windswept desert landscapes, an occasional sparse oasis of palm trees and lines of obedient camels. There were Bedouin style exotic tents. The camel jockeys were dressed in their vivid orange and royal purple robes, with large wrappings of colourful head dresses, and kohl eyeliner. It was one of the rare experiences that was exactly as I had expected. Due to the 100-plus degree (38-degree C) heat of the day, the camels travelled in the late part of the day.

The eight of us in our volunteer group had a fantastic time on the two-hour camel trek through the desert to our camp for the night. We took many photos, and laughed as the occasional camel got loose and 'free styled' it out of the pack to escape into the desert. Only to be rescued by a pissed off camel jockey.

Dinner was in the exotic Bedouin tents, sitting on local tribal rugs on the floor with small tables of food. Dinner was followed by a bonfire and the rest of the night was for viewing the spectacular display of stars in the desert sky. I have never seen such clarity to the stars. It was breathtaking.

The camel jockeys took the occasion, to also hit on all the beautiful young girls that were in our group, as well as pretty girls from other groups. When Alex and our volunteer girls were asked, "Do you want to go see my camel?" I assured them that I was escorting! The girls mentioned that of all the pick-up lines they have ever heard in their lives, "Do you want to come see my camel?" was one of the strangest.

Accompanied by me, the girls did go see the camels, as they were intriguing and cute. The camel jockeys became increasingly frustrated as I chaperoned. Eventually, they moved onto other girls to try to make them their wives for the night. I didn't see any takers on that one! But that was not before one of the camel jockeys asked me, "Would you take 2,000 camels in exchange for your daughter?"

"Not today," I replied, but check back next year!"

Morocco, Chefchaouen, 2016 – The Blue Village

Chefchaouen is a beautiful, small village in the Rio mountains, in the northwest of Morocco. Its origins date back to the 15th century. It is called by travel books 'The Blue City' because of its proliferation of blue trimmed houses, alleyways and doors. It is highly popular on social media. Many people think it is the most beautiful village in Morocco. It reminds me so much of some of the smaller villages on the Greek Islands, in that almost every home and business is coloured bright blue and white. It is an Instagram paradise and has gotten huge photo coverage in recent years.

Our eight-person group of travellers was excited to spend the weekend in Chefchaouen. I was in charge of finding a hostel and wanted to be sensitive to the budget restrictions of the group. I found a six dollar-a-night, per person, hostel on Hostelworld, and signed us up for an eight-person room. We arrived, threw our bags in the room and went out to explore the lovely town.

It wasn't until the next day that I noticed several, sketchy, unkempt, zoned out looking other travellers. Chefchaouen is also known as the 'Weed Capital' of Morocco. I didn't know that! It finally occurred to me that I had picked the cheapest hostel to book us in, and apparently so did all the drug addicts! The takeaway of this is, never book the cheapest place! Or your roommates will be the drug burnouts who also were looking for the cheapest lodging!

Morocco, Marrakech, 2016 – Finding a Beer

Marrakech is the fourth largest city in Morocco after Casablanca, Fez and Tangier. Its population is over a million people. It is a historic city, established in the 11th century, located 150 miles south of Casablanca. It's Medina, or ancient original fortressed city, is a UNESCO World Heritage Site. It is one of the busiest cities in Africa and boasts the largest traditional market in Morocco.

Over 10 million people visit Marrakech each year. The streets of the Medina are winding, confusing and yet charming, all at the same time. It looks as if little has changed here over the centuries. Winding through the Medina is a confusing, exhilarating, entertaining and often frustrating experience. The main streets are filled with shops with endless supplies of slippers, copper pots, rugs, shawls, trinkets, ceramics and everything else imaginable.

Finding the location of your lodging is virtually impossible, amongst the maze of houses and businesses. Using the services of an eager 12-year-old local boy's help is usually necessary. That is, for the extortion fee of three dollars. Or as Alex offered up, as she pointed to a donkey and his owner, "We can take the small taxi!"

The town centre of activity has been described as 'a world-famous square', and in the cooler evenings, is a circus of activity. Vibrant, colourfully lit restaurants, sandal shops, copper pot sellers, henna tattoo ladies, circus like performers, pickpockets and scoundrels all compete for tourist's money. The local people and endless array of characters are entertainment alone.

Just as you think finding anything is possible, you notice the absence of any beer, wine or alcohol. We are visiting during the most reverent month of the Muslim year, Ramadan. Abstaining from food and water during the daylight hours is the religious custom. And practicing Muslims do not drink alcohol at any point of the year. So, good luck finding a beer!

But it's hard to tell eight millennial volunteers to not pursue the illicit beer. After many inquiries, we were told to walk down a dark, creepy pathway to a, for lack of a better word, "Speak-easy" sort of a bar/restaurant. The host greeted us with a devious smile, and ushered us to a far reaching, back patio, hidden from all others.

This felt so incredibly surreal and ridiculous to go to this extent for the forbidden beverage! At the next table, a 30-year-old couple and some friends seemed to be thoroughly enjoying their alcoholic drinks. One of their female members was completely drunk and started belly dancing for their group.

We were treated like the deviant, sinners of the town, and the host was horrified as we ordered a second round of drinks. We all started to laugh and told stories of our real, deviant friends, and that actually we were on the tamer side of the 'wild' curve. As we, predominantly sober volunteers, made our way through the maze of the Medina to our hostel, we all agreed the 50-cent beer and crazy clubs of Cambodia were looking pretty good at this point!

Morocco, Rabat, 2016 – The Hammam

One way to experience a new, unique culture is to do a homestay. This can be a short term, like a locally cooked and served meal, up to staying with a family for the entire volunteer month. It is definitely a way to submerge yourself into the local culture.

Rabat is a traditional, very old town with its Medina, or ancient city, as the focal point of the town. The ancient houses and dwellings in the Medina looked like something from the 13th century, as its origin. The Medinas are often historical sites, and can't be altered from their original structure. There are narrow, winding, totally confusing streets in the Medina, and there are no cars or motorbikes. It has a relatively quiet atmosphere compared to the crazy traffic, honking horns and noisy trains just outside of the Medina.

Although it is easy to get lost in the Medina, you start to make mental notes of, left at the copper pot seller, right at the third spice guy, past the shoe merchant, and two blue doors down from the kebab seller. And you're home.

The six of us volunteers took over the ground floor of a four storey, what seemed to be, spacious home. The host family lived upstairs, which we were not invited to see the rest of the house. But with the open-air courtyard, we often heard lots of yelling, shouting and fighting many nights. It was of course in Arabic, but we guessed there was definitely some family drama going on.

The widowed mother of the home spoke little English, but was very gracious toward us. After a month of all of us calling her Momma, I found out she was three years older that I was! The women of the home also cooked the Iftar, the sundown, Ramadan meal for us most evenings.

The 35-year-old son seemed to be the breadwinner of the family, and sat with us many evenings. He loved to talk about himself incessantly, and must have figured we were fascinated with his boring life.

A few days after our arrival the mum asked us if we wanted to go to the Hammam. "Sure!" I said, having no clue what a Hammam is. Well, we would certainly find out! She collected our $10 each and we were off. After a few winding turns, but not too far from her home, we entered a cave like room. There was no sign, or anything that signified any kind of business. The inside was like an 'old school' locker room with baskets and hooks on the walls.

We were told to take off our clothes, but cover up with a towel. Modest Alex was getting nervous. We were instructed to go into a room that was tiled floor to ceiling that had some steam coming out of various spigots.

"Lay down," said one of the ladies, and we followed her command. She and another woman proceeded to throw buckets of water on us, wash our hair, and perform some type of simple massage. The two staff ladies, along with the other 12 females in the tiled room were completely naked, as were we.

Here in the land of the completely covered up society of Muslim Rabat, was the entire neighbourhood of naked neighbours. We thanked our God that it was women only!

A mortified Alex leaned her head sideways while getting doused with buckets of water and said, "Mum, this is the third weirdest thing I've ever done in my life!" I think I can wait a long time before I hear what the top two are!

Taiwan, Taipei, 1989 – Molly and the Explosion

Molly was a beautiful, tall, smart, college educated, 26-year-old from Albuquerque, New Mexico. Her shockingly long, blonde, hair and curvy, but slender figure, made many people compare her to the sports illustrated model sensation of the time, Christie Brinkley. Molly could stop traffic a block away, and break many young men's hearts!

She left quite a path of romantic destruction in her wake! The most enduring part of Molly was her unique and sweet personality. She truly had no idea how lovely and persuasive she was. She acted like a normal, non-beautiful person. Her father always said, "She could sell ice to the Eskimos!"

Molly was an adventurer at heart. She loved the exoticism of travel. After a short marriage and then a divorce, she decided to take time away from her job and see the world. She would start in Thailand. Molly travelled conservatively, as she did not have a lot of money saved for this trip. She knew she would need to work, at some point in the trip. She was a worker, and had a great work ethic.

She had a wonderful time traveling throughout Southeast Asia. She had no trouble meeting travel buddies and throngs of young guys drooled over this American Beauty. Then she met Brice! Brice was young, French and exotic! Brice usually dressed in a sarong, and had long, flowing, sun-kissed brown hair. Usually, a lack of a shirt, also. Brice could have easily been on the cover of dozens of romance novels. He seemed to be a younger version of Fabio, a romance novel cover darling, that also hawked margarine on TV commercials at that time.

Molly was smitten! The romance had made its way through Southeast Asia. As they travelled, money was becoming tight for the beautiful couple. Molly's idea was to go to Taiwan and start working to earn money. She was extremely marketable and knew she could get multiple jobs. The idea was to save up money to continue their travels.

Landing in Taipei, she was immediately hired to teach English to kids during the week days, supplemented by teaching English horseback riding, on the weekends to wealthy families. She was an excellent English dressage horseback rider and teacher. She also decided to work a few nights at a nearby bar/drinking establishment.

She would be the new St Paulie Beer Girl! She was costumed in a German dirndl skirt, laced low-cut blouse and her hair was in two braids on top of her head. She really did look like the young German maiden on the label. She was an instant hit!

What Molly didn't realise was that the beer hall she was working at was four floors high, with many, many tables of 10 people. It was mostly men imbibing after a long day of work. That was challenge enough. On her first evening, the first table of raucous Taiwanese men wanted to toast to her loveliness, her exactness of the beer label girl, and whatever else they could think of. Molly was no stranger to throwing down a few beers in her day!

By the second floor, she was feeling tipsy, and by the fourth floor, and many toasts, she was hammered! Somehow, she managed to do the beer girl job for four months, and it didn't damper her love of beer!

Busy working three jobs to save money, she was ragged with exhaustion. The big, Brice romance was not going so well. Although Brice was a nice guy, he was from a privileged family that did not instil a strong work ethic in him. The excuses were wearing thin, and his lack of motivation grew tiresome.

They lived on the third floor of a not glamorous apartment. Molly knew this was temporary housing and the intent was to save money.

Power cuts or power outages were common. On one occasion, she tried to plug in her hairdryer as she was getting ready for her evening job. Sparks flew and a puff of smoke, then darkness throughout the apartment.

She walked down the stairs to the building manager and explained in her best Mandarin, "We have had an explosion!"

The manager smiled broadly and shook his head and said "That is very, very good!"

Again, she explained, "We have had an explosion!" Still smiling, the man was now getting even more animated.

What is wrong with this guy, she thought! The confusion lasted many more minutes. It wasn't until a neighbour walked by who helped to translate the dire situation. The neighbour said, "Apparently, you told him you have just had a very big ejaculation, and he is congratulating you on your success!" Needless to say, Molly was mortified! She soon 'power cut' Brice out of her life.

Romania, Sibiu, 1995 – Molly and the Peace Corps

Thirty-two-year-old beautiful Molly, had successfully co-owned and ran a unique, kind of hippy-style, clothing store in Albuquerque, New Mexico. It was in a popular location near the University of New Mexico. It was successful, but she missed travelling and yearned for a bigger adventure than her hometown of Albuquerque could provide. With excellent references from her former jobs, she was accepted into the Peace Corps.

At that time the Peace Corps was a two-year commitment, and extremely hard to get accepted. To help ensure acceptance, she put a checkmark in the box that read 'Will go to any location'.

She was soon on her way to Sibiu, Romania, a city of about 150,000 people in the Transylvania area of the country, northwest of Bucharest. She was there to do a three-month intense Romanian language program before being placed in a smaller town, to help develop small businesses.

Armed with a positive attitude and a pocket guide to Romanian, she set out those first few days to get a feel for the lovely town. She was impressed with the politeness of the people and their willingness to let others go through a door, enter a bus and move to the side on a congested street.

But she wasn't sure she was hearing them correctly. It sounded like they were phonetically saying 'Fok U'. As one person motioned for the other to go first in the line. "No, Fok U," replied the other person. This went on all day and she saw one exchange after the other of the people saying what sounded like 'Fok U'. She was convinced this was the most polite cussing she had ever heard! Upon further studying, she learned they were simply instructing the other person to proceed first!

Laos, Central Laos, 2007 – Middle of Nowhere Small Village

While on a six-week tour of Southeast Asia, with a great company called Intrepid Travel, and nine other travellers, we stopped for a two-day homestay in a small village. I don't even remember the name of the village, but it had 200 people, and was located near the Mekong River. Intrepid Travel believes in the value of sustainable, local travel experiences. They pride themselves on helping out local communities and giving their travellers unique, non-tourist experiences. The company was recommended by many former Peace Corp volunteers.

The day before we arrived, we travellers were told that we would be going to the village and that they have about 40 kids. They suggested we get some books to read to the kids. Fortunately, we had three teachers in our group. So, the night before our visit, we were in a larger town and our group was buying candy, treats and books in their local language, as well as books in English. I decided a few soccer balls, and play balls would be fun too. We weren't sure how the difference in language was going to work out, but we'd give it our best try.

Our van pulled up and the village kids were so excited and curious to see all the big, strange, white people. Our guide spoke a little local language, and explained that we had gifts for them. The kids were beyond happy, and soon jacked up on all the sugary treats.

My travel buddy, my age and I, decided it was soccer time. We found an area to improvise a field and grabbed some rocks for goals. The kids watched intently, but had no idea what we were doing. We soon realised they had never seen a soccer ball and certainly didn't know what to do with the soccer ball.

With great care and patience, we pantomimed, the object of the game. We recruited a few other volunteers to help, and soon the village boys on the field were getting it. It was 95 degrees (35 degrees C), and massive humidity, but the fun continued. The bigger boys played; the little boys subbed in. It didn't matter what the score was or who was on which team. The kids were having a blast.

Over an hour and many goals later, we were ready for a break. I noticed that while the girls were having a good time reading with the travellers, none of the girls joined in the soccer games. Maybe the field was too big and scary.

So, I grabbed some of the older girls and a soccer ball. I made a smaller, less intimidating field, and threw someone's shoes down as the goal area. I again grabbed a female traveller and tried my best to explain how to play simplistic soccer. Soon the girls were off running and kicking the ball. I decided I would play goalie, and was happy to stand somewhat quietly in front of the makeshift goal.

We were so proud of the girl's enthusiasm and athleticism. They were having a great time. We were all having a great time. We were all quite the entertainment for the parents and family members of all the kids. The ball was heading my direction. About eight girls ran toward me. They kept running at me and we all ended up in a jumble, me at the bottom. Yow! My leg popped, and I immediately knew something was wrong.

The impact of all the girls had wrenched my leg and knee. It hurt like hell! I sat to the side as my injury swelled up. I couldn't move my knee. I later drank a few beers and gobbled some Tylenol.

My leg was a wreck and inoperable for the balance of the five weeks of the trip. But I still maintain, the girls didn't score on me on that play!

World Travel

Indonesia, China, Laos, Cambodia, India, Thailand, Sri Lanka, Morocco, Nepal, 2007-2018 – Volunteering with Underprivileged Kids

Travelling and volunteering with underprivileged kids and orphans in developing countries over the last 12 years, has taught me many things:

1. It doesn't take money to be happy.
2. The family or a substitute family unit is crucial to the continuing success of a kid.
3. These kids are innocent, curious, inquisitive, interested and eager to learn.
4. Underprivileged kids understand and believe that an education is a privilege.
5. These kids love and support each other.
6. Boys are universally competitive. Girls are universally nurturing.
7. The kids have a tremendous respect for elders and teachers.
8. Kids are creative and will use whatever resources available to them to problem solve, play, survive or just have fun.
9. The teenage kids do not have big aspirations or expectations for their future.
10. Music and more than one kid – Dance Party!

Thailand, Cambodia, Indonesia, Nepal, 2018 – The Future Dreams and Aspirations of the Underprivileged Kids

A common denominator I continue to run into in my travels and working with underprivileged kids, is the difference of the dreams and aspirations of the underprivileged kids, and how it differs from that of most Western kids.

In Thailand, the state school goes through tenth grade. Any education beyond that becomes a trade school or university. Many of the tenth-graders I taught told me their families didn't have money for furthering their education. When I asked them of their plans after school, many lowered their heads, looked down and they said they don't know. "Maybe work in a shop or with their parents," some of the kids would tell me.

I noticed the school did not have career counselling and didn't show an active attempt to help kids with available scholarships or creative ways to fund furthering their education.

Somehow, I had the sense these kids knew continuing their education was not going to happen. It was also a state school where many of the kids were being raised by grandparents. Many of the students' parents were not involved with their kids' lives due to jail, drugs, prostitution, abandonment or alcoholism.

Such realities were not spoken about, as it was just the circumstance that the grandparents were the primary caretakers. I witnessed many of these grandparents caring for their grandkids. I saw that the families were doing the best they could on limited financial resources.

I heard stories of many orphan girls that were taken out of the orphanage at about 16 years of age, by the mum who had placed them at the orphanage years before. The mum would come back to the orphanage and get their daughter, who would return to the family home to care for younger half siblings. I was told the girls were usually ambivalent toward the mother that had abandoned them.

I also saw worthy attempts, on the orphanage's part, to locate distant family members of orphans, in order to place them back in their communities, as they became beyond school age. The thought process was to re-acclimate the orphan to their village and culture, while trying to reconnect with any distant family members.

In Cambodia, amongst some of the poorest families, some of the students at Grace House Community Centre were getting sponsorship for furthering their education. This was the best example I have run across. The former students that I was volunteering with six years ago, were now college educated, or working on their college degrees, and were teaching at the Grace House School as teachers. It was all made possible through generous international donors and bright, hardworking students.

The concept of Grace House Community Centre is to help the entire community and family out, and help them overcome poverty. It is a smashing success. The biggest factor at Grace House is that all the classes are taught in English. These kids are spending half their day at their state school studying in Khmer, and the other half of the school day learning and studying in English.

These kids start in preschool learning English, and do not even realise they are bilingual. They learn to read, work on computers, do science, math and all subjects in English. The result being, they can easily converse with foreigners in English and get coveted jobs in the travel industry that requires good English skills.

I worked with two diverse groups of underprivileged kids in Bali. The first were village kids in after school English programs. These kids had parents, and lived in villages with extended families. Although, there was not a lot of income, the kids seemed to be well nourished, clean and happy. They ranged in age from preschool, age four, to sixth grade, age 14.

From being exposed to volunteers, they had some command of English, and could converse. I was lucky to teach in about five different classrooms and had lots of great adventures in learning, playing games, doing artwork and singing and dancing.

The elementary school 'after school programs' were optional for the kids and it was so great to see the active participation in so many kids choosing to spend their time learning and speaking English. It was great to see many of the younger siblings sneak into the class and participate, because they said, "It looks fun!" The kids that were 12-14 years old really did not talk about their future.

I learned from local young women that the path for a Balinese girl is usually to finish the 10th grade, then help the family make money by working. I was lucky to meet some of the more educated young ladies that were attending college. They were the first generation of women in their families to achieve a higher education, and they all spoke English very well. They had aspirations of working in the tourism business.

In the Balinese culture, most women do not drive and they are not considered for tour guide jobs. Those jobs are considered masculine, and left for the males. The women's jobs tend to be more in the hospitality section of tourism.

As I talked more to the young ladies who were pursuing an education, their thoughts about the future were primarily about marriage and a family. There was a lot of talk and giggling about which of the local young men they thought were handsome and nice. It seems to be a universal conversation for young ladies!

The second group of kids I spent months with in Bali, were orphan kids age 3-18. These kids are fantastic, loving, smart and ever so appreciative for any volunteers who spend time with them and donate supplies.

I am well aware of the current backlash of certain TED Talk speakers and other millennials, telling people not to give money to orphanages. They preach that corruption and misappropriation of funds are problems, so they recommend abstaining from donating to orphanages. I challenge these advocates to spend time with kids who need help, and to research further into well run orphanages.

In Cambodia, I sat through a seminar of one such millennial. She spent over an hour telling the 25 of us, mainly volunteers, that she wants to put a stop to donations to orphanages. She was full of fire and brimstone about all the corruption that goes on in the orphanages.

Question and answer time became quite feisty, when a man in his 60s, sitting behind me, asked her what plan she would recommend to the 36 orphaned kids he has cared for over 20 years. I secretly chuckled, because she had no plan!

Another of the issues she spoke about is the feeling the orphan kids get with a rotation of volunteers. I feel I have a very experienced opinion on that issue after twelve years volunteering with these kids. My feeling is that 'yes', these kids form attachments to volunteers, and the volunteers leave. Some would say that that is a traumatic abandonment of the orphans each time. I liken it somewhat to kids with biological families. They too, have teachers, coaches, religious leaders, scout leaders that cycle through their lives. But I have not heard that called abandonment.

A good rule of many volunteer organisations is to spend at least a month volunteering with kids, if possible. It creates a bond and a familiarity. It is also true that many volunteers repeat their placements with orphan and underprivileged kids. I feel it reassures the kids that they are important enough for the volunteer to come back. My daughter, Alex, and I have repeated seven volunteer placements between the two of us.

The most amazing part is the look of excitement and astonishment on their faces when you arrive back to see them. Some of the now, over 18-year-old kids, follow my daughter on social media, and she has met with them in their countries and continues to be involved in their lives. They both feel a real friendship and concern for each other's lives.

Travel Rules, 2018 — Be Safe, Be Smart!

After living in New York City for 18 years, and traveling the globe most of my life, I have developed some safety rules that have served me well while traveling in foreign countries:

1. Travel lightly! The traveller who is bogged down by luggage, loose bags, cameras and too much stuff, is a target for a thief. It also slows you down in all aspects of travel. Streamline your wardrobe, shoes and cameras to what I call run for the train, bus, camel, tuk tuk, boat, plane, ability!

2. Do not drink excessively at night! You will become an instant target for bad things to happen, and you will be extremely vulnerable.

3. Nothing good happens after midnight! Remember what your mum used to say! Whether or not you are drinking, again, you will be a target for theft, or worse!

4. Day drink instead. Have your fun and drinks at lunch or an early dinner. You'll have a much less chance of safety problems, as the thugs prefer to work at night.

5. When possible, have a travel buddy or buddies with you. This way you can look out for each other. And stick together.

6. Split up your debit/credit cards and cash in different purses, backpacks or a money belt. Use the hotel room, locked safe. Carry a sturdy, small, across the shoulder travel purse or around the neck passport/money holder. Don't make it easy for a purse snatcher.

7. Make several copies of your passport, photo and information page, debit/credit cards, insurance information, lodging information and anything else you feel is important. Place a copy in two or more locations. That way, if a bag is lost or stolen, you still have access to your documents. I do not keep a photocopy of the back of credit/debit cards in the same place, as it could be stolen and used immediately by a hacker.

8. If a situation seems sketchy, it probably is! Trust your instincts and trust your gut. Being led down a dark alley to see some rugs, fake designer bags, cheap T-shirts, gold jewellery or anything else sketchy isn't worth the risk of getting mugged or robbed.
9. At night in bars, be very careful ordering cocktails. Some clubs have reputations of drugging cocktails. Ordering a beer, or drink from a bottle is a bit safer. And watch them open the top if possible.
10. Try to use legitimate transportation drivers. A metred taxi, public boat, bus, van, car, Uber, ferry, or tuk tuk will reduce the occurrence of a safety issue when there is a company and driver associated with the transportation. As cheap as the other form of transportation sounds, it's risky. Use metred taxis when possible. It keeps the price per ride legitimate.

Traditional Costumes – Ladies, Don't Do It!

One of my favourite travel rules is 'Girlfriends DO NOT let girlfriends buy traditional costumes while travelling!' As much as you get caught up in the moment in China and think the traditional cheongsam red dress, that beautiful Chinese women wear so elegantly, will translate to your world when you get home, you are wrong!

The German pinafore dress that you so carefully picked out, with its tightly laced bodice and dirndl skirt will not ever see daylight after the crazy Octoberfest weekend!

All the time spent in the New Delhi shop, while sales attendants fuss over the intricate folding of your new, overpriced sari, will too, not get put to good use at home. Yes, you will be the hit foreigner at the local Indian wedding, and you will look smashing for the event, but good luck walking into a Western wedding wearing your prized sari.

Another tempting fate is the going to the tailors of Hoi An, Vietnam and think you are going to end up with a high-end designer dress that looks like it's just off the runway of the best designers in the world. If you're just looking for a fun, cheap, low expectation garment, then go for it! But if you think these folks can translate your perceived fashion ideas into your fashion runway dreams then keep your expectations low.

I had an experience with my travel buddies in those same tailoring shops in Hoi An, Vietnam. I passed on having the tailors make a garment for me, but the other six girls were so excited to have their design ideas, created into fashion fantasy. I sat and watched as they excitedly previewed fabrics, trims, buckles, and linings.

My first sign of horror was when a shop worker pulled out a fashion magazine from 20 years ago. "You like?" she said to my buddies. They didn't seem to be as bothered as I was that their frame of Western fashion was 20 years old. As final details were decided, each of the girls was measured and left a deposit. "Come back tomorrow at this time," said the owner. I couldn't dare burst their excitement, of owning a custom-made garment.

Yes, the next day we returned and the fashions were DREADFUL!!! Some fit and were dreadful, others didn't even fit and were worse. We did what we always did in times of crisis, went to the bar and drank! After many drinks I made each girl raise their hand and repeat after me, "Girlfriends do not let girlfriends buy traditional dresses, or get one made!"

The best experience of traditional costumes, that are actually beautiful, is in Bali. Many of the temples require women to be modestly covered up. In Bali that means a sarong. For religious ceremonies and weddings, the local Balinese women wear four items. A sarong, called a kamen. The sarong, is a long strip about six feet (two metres) of usually bright batik fabric that is wrapped around the waist. There are appropriate lengths of the garments and appropriate instructions how to tie it tightly around the tops of the thighs, so the bottom is encased.

The blouse is called a kebab. It is a sheer intricately embroidered cotton, nylon or polyester lace with a solid colour corset underneath. It has long sleeves and must come past the wristband to be fashionable. A short-sleeve top is considered unfashionable. Each item, and its way of wearing it, dictates the woman's level of chic. Girls who wear a lace blouse with a low 'V' front, may use it as a way to attract male attention.

The outfit is finished off with two colourful sashes called kebaya. It serves to hold up the sarong, as well as often pulled tightly to enhance the body, as a corset.

Historically, the dress constrains women's movement, and restricts them into taking small, feminine steps. To run, as a Balinese woman, is considered unflattering. Their gender ideals require them to be passive and modest. The culture is, that a woman must wait for a man to court her, and it is not appropriate to actively attract a man's attention, or pursue him.

As my 10 volunteer travel girls and I were on our way to a beautiful water temple in Bali, our local female guide patiently helped us wrap, bind, tie and wiggle into our traditional costumes for our water experience. I have to say the ladies looked lovely, and it would be quite possible for them to recreate that look at home on a hot summer evening with a colourful drink in their hand. Of course, they would be having thoughts of beautiful Bali!

I always have to laugh at what I call 'elephant pants' These are the $2 elastic waist, ankle length, usually black, and white print staple of both male and female travellers. It is often accompanied by the obligatory 'Beer T-shirt'. These, usually young travellers, somehow seem to think they are worldly and fashionable in their local outfit. I hate to break the bad news to them, but it really screams, "I haven't done my laundry lately, so I have to wear this ridiculous costume!"

I have laughed many times at Halloween time when I see on social media, photos of my travel girls, dressed up for the night in their Octoberfest dirndls with tight hair braids and large glass mug of beer. The occasional girl in her red silk, tightly fitting Chinese cheongsam, with obligatory chopsticks in her hair, and high black pointy shoes. Then there is the exotic glittering sari that the girl spent an hour looking at YouTube to figure out how to correctly, or practically wrap her sari, so as to have it not fall off.

Again, I repeat, "Girlfriends do not let girlfriends buy traditional costumes!"

Volunteering, 2018 – Go, Volunteer, Make a Difference!

This book is meant to inspire people to volunteer! I am no stranger to volunteering. In addition to being a business person, I have done a lifetime of volunteering. It is an important and innate part of my life. I get immense joy out of helping people and creating positive moments, as well as a human connection.

I have taught and encouraged my grown children to incorporate voluntarism into their lives. Memories of my three-year-old daughter sitting in a stroller handing candy canes out to homeless folks in Tucson Arizona, make me smile. She was told by one tired, scruffy, nice homeless man, "You are a little angel."

After the encounter, every time I would get mad at her she would remind me, "You can't get mad at me, I'm an angel!"

I taught my kids that the human connection was as important as handing people in need, warm hats, socks, toothbrushes and toiletries. Soup kitchens were available for food, but most of the homeless we encountered, needed warm clothes and personal care items. My kids became quite good at our adventures helping people. They happily handed out the items we had gathered up, to folks, far worse off than we were. We often had school friends and families join us. This expanded our reach to be able to help more people, as well as involve my kid's more privileged friends.

We always started with a list of what items we knew were needed and appreciated. Each time, we learned which items were the most popular and drew the biggest smile.

Books seemed to be a hit, as the folks sitting at the parks all day certainly had a lot of free time.

We gathered lots of books from our shelves at home and from our friends, to give away. As my son, Benjie and his buddy, Bennett, were handing out books, one young homeless man remarked "Oh, I've read almost all of those!" It made the boys realise that being homeless didn't mean uneducated.

Another time an older man asked Benjie if he had a Bible. "Oh, yeah!" he said as he ran to our car to get his Bible out of the side pocket of the car door. Younger sister, Alex ran to the car too, and produced her Bible. They handed them over to the man and he was delighted! I later realised that my kids wanted to unburden themselves with their Bibles, so they didn't have to read them for Religious Ed class. It was a bit self-serving. It was hard for the religion teacher to argue when my kids said "I gave my Bible away to a homeless man!"

At a particularly lean economic time, I was determined to make sure we continued our tradition of helping the homeless. I thought long and hard about how we could help the greatest numbers of people, with the limited budget I had.

One way, was always with soda, cookies and bakery treats. I was always armed with lots of litres of soda, cookies and cupcakes. I always had myself and all the kids join in the treats, as unbeknownst to them, they were learning that we are all equal. I taught my kids how to talk with homeless folks. I told them to ask questions, and talk about various topics like sports, music, and the weather. Also, ask questions about where they were from, their families, animals and favourite foods. In high school, my daughter used to bring her spirited husky dog, while we handed out brown bags of food. Fuzzy was always a big conversation starter.

The conversations were very lively and my kids heard several stories about the homeless folks' lives, including their incarcerations, drugs of choice, gang member information and the proud display of their tattoos!

One group of proud tattooed gang members patiently posed for photos for my daughter's photo journalism class project. One woman also explained to my kids that she was a prostitute. These experiences have been invaluable to my kids and they have an innate ability to talk to people from the CEO level to that tattooed, recently paroled gang-member.

Volunteering, 2018 – An Experience of a Lifetime!

I love the spirit, enthusiasm, idealism, hard work, dedication and innovativeness of the volunteers. These are generally millennials, with an exception of some retired people, who are on some kind of a break between chapters of their very interesting lives.

In my experience, the volunteers are 90% female, average age 24, and extremely smart young people. I find the volunteers that I have worked with are generally from England, Australia, the Netherlands, USA, Canada, Japan, Ireland, France, New Zealand, Sweden, Brazil, Scotland, Mexico and other countries. The common denominator is that the volunteers all speak English.

There is tremendous amount of camaraderie and a recognition of 'like-minded' individuals among the volunteers. It is one of the few groups of people that I have ever been around, where there seems to be no sense of competition. I've seen all ages get along fantastically, and all join in, to help out!

Each volunteer is there to help the cause, whether it is teaching underprivileged kids English, teaching art, sports, music, saving turtles, building toilets or painting classrooms. I have been privileged to volunteer with hundreds of these fantastic people.

Some of the best stories I know, are the volunteers 'lost in translation' stories. There seems to be a 'work hard, play hard' mentality amongst the volunteers, as they are using their own, precious time and money to volunteer. Another common denominator of the volunteers is a sense of adventure, thrill seeking and a large amount of fearlessness! The non-work hours and weekends are filled with their own set of hilarious stories and adventures.

Motorbike crashes, hangovers, bug bites, sunburns, blisters, diarrhoea, and massive hangovers seem to be the norm. Although, they are usually offset by beautiful waterfalls, stunning temples, sunrises at the top of mountains, wonderful local celebrations, stunning diving, beautiful religious ceremonies, and local sports adventures. And the plentiful alcohol, contributing to the hangovers!

This is all before the unbelievably great feeling of helping a kid learn English, do math problems, kick a ball, blow bubbles, do artwork, and learn something they didn't know when they came to class! I have the utmost respect for all volunteers who leave their country, spend their own time and money and walk into a situation where few speak the local language, and help people in need.

On many occasions I have talked a volunteer or several, down from that seventh shot of tequila, kissing the local playboy, eating the stick full of unidentifiable insects, dancing on the platform, letting the delegates from the Democratic Republic of Congo buy them drinks, jumping off the big cliff, or putting three or more on a motorbike. And I claim to have the final approval on any tattoos!

My volunteers have come to love me as their 'Temporary Mum'. I have held back hair and rubbed the backs of many girls as they throw up that seventh shot, had their hearts broken, or tried to buy that ugly traditional costume. I tell them to let their mums know that I'm looking out for their precious cargo! Their mums just don't need to know the gory details!

For many volunteers working with kids, a weekly lice shampoo treatment is a common occurrence, as a huge number of kids have lice. The kids too, do lice treatments, but irradiating lice is difficult in many of the overcrowded environments they live in. A bandana and hair pulled up in a bun is the volunteer hairstyle of choice, as well as necessity!

I am so privileged to have worked with such an amazing group of volunteer young people. It is great to see their lives unfold on social media. The engagements, weddings, kids, grandkids and family celebrations are a great way to still feel connected to everyone. My son, Benjie, and I were thrilled when Jenny Mycock got married and took her new husband's name!

Volunteering, 2018 – My Inspiration

My choice of volunteering is with underprivileged kids. I live in a world where the majority of kids I have known are privileged. I have worked hard to show my own kids the reality of many of the world's kids, the less fortunate ones.

I want to inspire people to be creative and volunteer in an area of their interests and love. Help out at an animal shelter, plant trees, spend time with the elderly. Help at a hospital, soup kitchen, after school program, medical centre or help with fun runs. Mow the elderly neighbour's lawn, teach a single mum's kid how to ride a bike, help a refugee learn English or help to save the whales. Become a 'big brother, big sister' to a kid in need, and spend time with that child. My challenge is to inspire people to do something to help someone or something out!

From joining the Peace Corps to helping the elderly blind man cross the street, the rewards of volunteering are infinite! When I volunteer, teaching English with kids, I am rewarded with hundreds of hugs and smiles. I can't recall any other job I've ever had had like it. The measure of my success is if that kid can do one thing at the end of the day better than he could when he came to school. The day is then a success!

Sometimes, volunteering means, just being compassionate and listening to someone. Being concerned, caring and engaging in conversation, can also be rewarding. I have always found that a person will grow and learn many life lessons by volunteering.

If a child sees his or her parent volunteering early in their life, and participates, it is highly likely that volunteering will become a part of the child's life as they grow up. My 22-year-old daughter, Alex, has been my volunteer travel buddy for 10 years. All of her hard work, sacrifice, dedication, loving and caring for the many, many orphans and underprivileged kids we have worked with over the years, has definitely paid off. She was chosen over hundreds of applicants to intern at National Geographic Travel in the digital marketing department. After graduating from University of Alabama recently, she was offered a full-time position and is currently delighted to be working there!

If I can inspire one or more people to 'go, volunteer! Make a difference!' Then I have succeeded.

My year of volunteering, helping underprivileged kids, does not stem from a need to find myself. I found myself long ago! I am not in search of any spiritual enlightening or searching for Nirvana. I am comfortable with a lifetime of my own religion. I'm not looking to have thousands of Instagram followers. I don't care about social media. Simply put, I just want to help kids!

USA, Tucson, Arizona, 2010-2018 — My Kids and International Volunteering

Fifteen-year-old Alex and I were on a plane to Siem Reap, Cambodia eight years ago to volunteer. I was determined to expose my kids to more volunteering experiences than just their hometown. My son, Benjie, had volunteered a year earlier, through his high school program. The excellent school teacher annually brought senior level kids to teach English in a small village in north Kenya.

The semester before the trip, he and his 14 classmates studied East African Studies. They learned about local customs, etiquette, geography, teaching skills and some language skills. While in Kenya, the kids 'team taught' in the sparse, meagre, dusty classrooms. Some of the students walked two miles to their schools, and if they were lucky, maybe had a bicycle to use.

Benjie came back with many exciting stories, and the classmates had definitely had the experience of a lifetime. Benjie noticed that the young kids at his school were playing soccer with a rolled-up wad of paper held together by duct tape. It didn't seem to worry the local kids, but it broke Benjie's heart that they didn't even have one ball to play with. He told me that later he went to the market, and bought a soccer ball.

The next day he told all the kids to gather around him, as he hid the ball from them. He then said, "Look up!" As he threw the ball in the air. He said the kids all screamed with delight! He said he never knew the impact of a $2 ball until that day.

One of the volunteer classmates came to the group and told a story of a boy who could no longer attend class, as his parents didn't have money for school. The volunteer kids asked how much was needed to keep the boy in school for the year. "About $240," the volunteer teacher of the boy said. Each of the USA kids went to their bunk, and threw in a $20 bill. They had made a direct difference in that kid's life!

I'm not sure if the other parents noticed as I did, but I had an extremely thankful, appreciative, caring kid that stepped off that plane from Kenya!

Volunteering Reflection, 2017-2018

This past year, I have been robbed, broken my leg, had seven bank cards stolen, had two motorbike crashes, and recently experienced six earthquakes. I have been extorted for money by the police, had my clothes stolen, been incessantly stared at, had my backpack lost and had my Apple ID compromised several times. If that weren't enough, I have had hundreds of mosquito bites, many bouts of diarrhoea and am the punchline of many local jokes! Oh, and 99% of what the locals are saying, I do not understand.

But I would not trade one moment for the incredibly rewarding year I have had, volunteering in Thailand,

Cambodia, Indonesia and Nepal. If that is price I have to pay to help underprivileged kids out, then I'm in!

I've been in a world of extreme heat and humidity, little to no air conditioning, water that is undrinkable, beds that resemble box springs, WI-FI that may or probably doesn't work, food I can't pronounce, let alone, figure what it's made of. I have forgotten what ice cubes look like, and I can barely recall what cold beer tastes like. It has been a long time since I saw a refrigerator. My perfume of choice is 99% DEET mosquito spray.

I have been on every conceivable form of transportation from tuk tuk, cyclo, river raft, plane, rickety fishing boat, overnight train, busses with chickens next to me, motorbikes, ferryboat, rickety bicycles, houseboat, local busses, cars, jeeps, vans, subways and more.

I have been sick more times this year than I have in the past ten years, with everything from colds, passed on from the kids, to a broken leg and far too many hospital visits. I was determined to continue the year of volunteering, no matter what setbacks I had incurred, including the less than wonderful conditions.

My lack of luxury and discomfort did not dampen my spirit! I would always take a moment to remember that the kids that I was privileged to work with, did not have any luxuries. How could I possible complain about a lack of air conditioning, food, or hard bed, when I knew I had it far better than the kids did. I have always used my travels to the third world to help remind myself of how good I have it!

Every day I am grateful for my life! I have had the most interesting, rewarding year of my life! I am so fortunate that I am healthy, educated, have two great kids, and a fantastic family and friend support system. If I can help out kids in need, and inspire others to volunteer, then I have accomplished my goal!

Indonesia, Bali, 2018 – Bali-Travel Review, What I Have Learned

I am no stranger to traveling and volunteering in developing countries. I have been volunteering for four to six weeks each summer for the past 12 years, as well as this entire, last year. I have been fortunate to meet thousands of wonderful local kids and adults.

I have been a part of so many wonderful teachable moments, crazy experiences, heartfelt conversations, ceremonies, celebrations, problem solving, health concerns, sharing, trusting, wiping tears, and sometimes just helping a kid get through the day!

After raising two of my own kids, who are millennials, my opinion is that 'kids are kids!' This is regardless of the financial situation their families are in. The 1,200 underprivileged kids I was fortunate enough to work with this past year have taught me many things.

I firmly believe kids need a family structure to thrive in. If the child is an orphan, their family becomes the many other orphans, as well as the caretakers at the orphanage. Some of the most caring, loving, gentle people I have ever met are these caretakers. They seem to have an unusually high amount of love, patience, dedication and caring to give to the kids.

I also witnessed that among the daily chaos of running an orphanage, there is never enough money, resources or time to meet all the needs of the many kids. Unfortunately, most orphanages do not get any funding from the government, and must rely on donations to survive. This stretches the human resources of the orphanages, as fundraising can be a full-time job.

Usually the caretakers are not qualified, or exceptionally good at fundraising. And they do not have the time in their day. As the fundraisers may or may not be the best at childcare, it takes a team of both to run an orphanage.

Although the orphanages I volunteered with served healthy, nutritious food, there was no money for anything extravagant at meal time. The diets consisted mainly of rice, vegetables, and small amounts of meat or tofu. Water was the only drink I saw. Occasionally, there were small amounts of milk. Interestingly enough, I did not witness any food allergies amongst any of the orphans. There were no processed, expensive snacks, ice cream or sweets. When volunteers brought candy or sweet treats, it was quite thrilling for the kids.

I have experienced, kids of all countries, have an inherent love of learning, curiosity, eagerness to please, respect for authority figures, kindness toward others. They look for approval and acceptance from their family or substitute family structure.

Sometimes there are cracks in the system that produce kids that have behavioural issues, distrust authority, feel hopeless, and are bullies. Some of the kids come from abusive situations at home, and many have witnessed horrific situations. I did encounter some of these kids. Although, I am not professionally trained in these areas, I did my best to work with the kids. Sometimes that meant getting the shy student out on the sports field, where they can display their talent. Or help a kid do an art project or drawing, which brings out their talents. Sometimes a kid excelled at helping to cook meals, or tending to a garden.

I worry about all the wonderful kids and their futures, like every mother does. I know I can't fix everything, I only hope and pray for the best. I'll do what I can.

I am convinced, after spending 12 summers and this past year volunteering with underprivileged kids and orphans in developing nations, that the key to helping them is to raise money to help educate these kids!

So I will be spending the rest of my life raising money to help educate the underprivileged kids and orphans! Thank you for coming along with me on my crazy journey!

All of the kids' names have been changes to protect their identities, and some of the adults' names have been changed. You will know who you are!

SAWASDEE KHA!
LEE HI!
SELAMAT MALAM!
NAMASKAR